THE STRUGGLE IS REAL

A Journey of Faith, Freedom, and Fierce Resilience

Discover How to Build
Fierce Resilience
and Turn Every
Setback Into a Comeback!

LAVERN CARR

THE STRUGGLE IS REAL. Copyright © 2025. Lavern Carr. All Rights Reserved.

No rights claimed for public domain material, all rights reserved. No part of this publication may be reproduced, stored in a retrieval system, or transmitted in any form or by any means, electronic, mechanical, photocopying, recording, scanning, or otherwise, without the prior written permission of the publisher. Violation may be subject to civil or criminal penalties.

ISBN: 978-1-965635-83-4 (paperback)

Printed in the United States of America

THE STRUGGLE IS REAL

A Journey of Faith, Freedom, and Fierce Resilience

"The Struggle Is Real" is more than a story—it's a testimony. In these pages, Lavern invites you into the quiet valleys and triumphant peaks of her journey—a life shaped by faith, tested by fire, and refined by resilience. It's a journey of growth, grit, and God's unshakable guidance—a reminder that every setback can become a setup for strength.

My Grandma

LAVERN CARR

Dedication

To every woman who has ever walked through the fire and questioned whether she would make it out alive, this book is for you.

To the sisters, mothers, and grandmothers whose stories of quiet strength, resilience, and unwavering faith have shaped generations, you are the heartbeat of this journey.

To my friends and loved ones who stood beside me through the darkest nights, reminding me that even in pain, love remains real; I dedicate these pages to you with gratitude and affection.

Above all, to God, who transformed my pain into purpose and my trials into triumphs. May every word in these pages stand as a testament to Your unfailing grace and redeeming power.

Acknowledgement

No story is ever written alone. This book is the product of countless hands that held me, voices that spoke life into me, and hearts that refused to let me give up when the weight of the world felt too heavy.

First and foremost, I give all glory and praise to God, my constant strength, my healer, and guide. Without His grace, none of this would have been possible.

To my beloved grandmother, whose wisdom and love shaped the foundation of who I am, thank you for teaching me resilience, compassion, and the power of forgiveness. Your words still echo in my heart.

To my uncle, who believed in me when I doubted myself; your support gave me the courage to keep moving forward.

To Ms. Quen, my dearest friend and sister by choice, thank you for walking beside me through sleepless nights, endless challenges, and moments of doubt. Your friendship reminded me that I was never alone.

To every friend, mentor, teacher, and soul who encouraged me along this journey, your kindness lit the path during my darkest days.

To Ellecia Clarke, my book coach at *The Writer's Perch,* thank you for your support and guidance. The completion of this book would not have been possible without your encouragement and expertise.

Finally, to every woman who will read these pages and see a reflection of her own story, this book is for you. May it remind you that no matter how heavy the struggle, you are stronger than you think, braver than you know, and destined for more than you can imagine.

Table of Contents

Dedication v
Acknowledgement vii
Introduction 15

Part A
My Journey of Faith and Resilience

Chapter 1: Roots of Resilience 19
    My Life in the Village 19
    A Grandmother's Strength and Sacrifice 20
    Lessons of Resilience and Gratitude 21

Chapter 2: Lessons In Discipline And Determination 25
    A Time of Achievement and Joy 25
    Lessons in Humility and Discipline 26
    The Blessing of Prayer and Guidance 27
    Graduation, Leadership, and New Beginnings 28

Chapter 3: A New Horizon: Lessons in Courage and Resilience 31
    Life Lessons Beyond the Classroom 32
    Discovering Strength and Resilience 33

Chapter 4: Lessons in Life, Loss, and Love 35
    Morning Strength and Daily Resilience 35
    Facing Loss and Life's Fragility 36

Survival, Gratitude, and True Happiness 38

Chapter 5: Trials, Trust, and Lessons in Provision 41

    Choosing My Path Amidst Financial Hurdles 41

    Disappointment and Finding Small Blessings 42

    Desperation and the Lessons of Trust 43

Chapter 6: Foundations, Loss, and Reclaiming My Future 45

    The End of Childhood and a Firm Roof 45

    The Fragility of Dependence 46

    New Opportunities and the Power of Self-Reliance 47

Chapter 7: A Key of My Own 49

    Unlocking My First Sanctuary 49

    Rejection and the Road to Independence 50

    A New Home, A New Beginning 51

Chapter 8: Love, Loss, and Lessons in Truth 53

    A Car, a Choice, and a Costly Mistake 53

    A Love That Was Deception 54

    Choosing Myself Again 55

Chapter 9: Love, Responsibility, and the Unseen Hand of Grace 57

    A Light Walks into My Life 57

    Love That Came with Roses 58

    Family Trials and Unshaken Faith 59

    Flashback – The Car That Stole My Peace 60

Chapter 10: Driving Through Fear - Roads That Shape Us 63

    Learning the Roads, Learning Myself 63

    Trials, Dangers, and the Hand of God 64

Chapter 11: Loss, Resilience, and the Power of Inner Strength 69
    Moments of Beauty Amidst Life's Storms 69
    Grief, Justice, and the Strength Within 70

Chapter 12: When Doors Close, Greater Ones Open 73
    A Doorway to Canada and Lessons in Resilience 74
    A Journey of Faith: Finding Strength In Foreign Places 75

Chapter 13: Returning, Rebuilding, and Rising Stronger 79
    Finding Your Inner Strength 79
    The Power of Starting Again 81

Chapter 14: New Paths, New Promises 85
    Pursuing the Path of Care 85
    A Complete Change in Life Trajectory 86

Chapter 15: Trials That Shape Resilience 89
    The Grief of Losing a Loved One 89
    When New Opportunities Arise 92
    Lessons of Compassion and Courage 93

Chapter 16: The Courage to Keep Moving Forward 97
    Rising Through the Seasons 97
    A New Chapter of Learning 98
    Faith, Friendship, and Finding Strength 99

Chapter 17: The Legacy of a Life Well Lived 101
    Lessons that Shape the Soul 101

Part B

The Five Pillars of Fierce Resilience

Chapter 18: A Framework for Unshakeable Strength and Unstoppable Faith 107
    Resilience – The Power to Rise Again 107
    When Life Knocks You Down 108
    What Resilience Really Looks Like 108
    The Transformation in the Struggle.. 109
    You Are Living Proof... 110
    Introducing the Five Pillars of Fierce Resilience 110

The Five Pillars of Fierce Resilience: A Framework for Unshakeable Strength and Unstoppable Faith

Pillar 1: Faith Beyond Feelings – Anchoring Your Soul in the Storm
    When Faith Feels Hard 114
    Faith Is a Muscle, Not a Mood 114
    Faith and Reality Can Coexist 115
    How to Strengthen Faith Beyond Feelings 115
    Faith in Action 116
    Closing Thought 117

Pillar 2: Courage in Chaos – Standing Firm When Life Falls Apart 119
    Courage Doesn't Cancel Fear, It Rises Above It........................ 119
    The Lesson Hidden in Chaos 120
    The Courage to Let Go 121
    How to Build Courage in Chaos 121
    Real Courage is Quiet 122
    Closing Thought 123

Pillar 3: Wisdom Through Waiting – Learning to Trust Divine Timing 125
    The Silent Classroom of Waiting 125
    The Purpose of the Pause 126
    Learning to Live in the In-Between 126
    Patience as a Superpower 127
    How to Gain Wisdom Through Waiting 128
    What Waiting Reveals 129
    Closing Thought 130

Pillar 4: Grace for Growth – Becoming Better, Not Bitter 133
    The Breaking That Builds You 133
    The Gift of Self-Compassion 134
    The Power of Perspective 135
    How to Grow with Grace 136
    When Growth Gets Lonely 137
    Closing Thought 140

Pillar 5: Purpose Through Pain – Turning Wounds into Wisdom . 141
    The Refining Power of Pain 142
    Finding Purpose in What Tried to Break You 142
    From Pain to Power: How to Transform Your Story .. 143
    Lessons from the Journey 145
    Closing Thought 146
    Final Reflection: The Five Pillars Of Resilience Summarized For Daily Reading 150

Why I Wrote This Book 153
About the Author 155

Introduction

Life has a way of testing us in ways we never expect. Sometimes the struggles are silent, hidden behind a smile; other times they are loud, raw, and undeniable. For many of us, the journey has been filled with heartbreak, loss, betrayal, and moments where the weight of it all felt unbearable. Yet, here we stand. Bruised perhaps, but unbroken. Scarred maybe, but still rising.

This book, *The Struggle Is Real*, is more than my story; it is our story. It is the voice of every woman who has ever cried herself to sleep, wiped away her tears in silence, and still got up the next morning to fight another day. It is a testament to survival, resilience, and the unshakable truth that no matter how dark life becomes, there is always light waiting to break through.

I did not write this book to simply retell my hardships. I wrote it because within every struggle, there is a lesson. Within every setback, there is an opportunity. Within every storm, there is strength being built that we cannot yet see. My journey—filled with trials, triumphs, and transformation—is a mirror to remind you that you are not alone, and that your story matters too.

The world is filled with women who have been silenced, overlooked, or made to feel powerless. But I believe that when we share our stories, we unlock healing not only for ourselves but also for those who are walking the same path. This is why I dare to tell mine.

In Part A, you will walk with me through my story; my childhood, challenges, and the moments that shaped me.

Part B of this book goes a step further: it introduces the **5 Pillars of Fierce Resilience**, a framework designed to help you cultivate **unshakable strength and unstoppable faith**. These pillars are tools, lessons, and guiding principles drawn from my life, crafted to empower you to rise above your struggles, transform your pain into purpose, and walk boldly into your fullest potential.

As you read these pages, I want you to see yourself, not just in my pain, but in my victories. I want you to feel hope rise inside of you, reminding you that your best days are not behind you, but ahead. I want you to be empowered to take off the masks, face your truth, and walk boldly into the fullness of who you were created to be.

So let us begin this next chapter together. The struggle is real, but so is your strength, purpose, and power to overcome.

Welcome to a story of survival. Welcome to a story of resilience. Welcome to a story that might just awaken something inside of you.

Part A

My Journey of Faith and Resilience

Chapter 1

Roots of Resilience

MY LIFE IN THE VILLAGE

Growing up in a small village was never easy. Life was hard, and it was rough. The village where I was raised was so quiet that at night the only sounds were the chirping of crickets and the call of the peeny wallie. It was so still that if you dropped a pin, you could hear it echo.

I remember vividly one story my grandmother told me. She said that one day, my mother took me away to a place called Content: another village in Jamaica. But my grandmother came for me the very same day. She couldn't bear the thought of me living there. She always wanted the best for me, and she loved me with a depth I can hardly explain—more than she loved herself.

By the age of seven, I had already learned how to cook, wash, and do almost every chore a household required. My grandmother kept a small pen where she raised chickens, pigs, and goats. One morning, though I was not feeling well, she insisted I get up to look after the animals. She reminded me that the animals were the reason we could go to school, the reason we survived, and the reason we ate. So, no matter how tired or unwell we felt, we got up and did what had to be done.

A GRANDMOTHER'S STRENGTH AND SACRIFICE

There were two other girls in our home. One of them was adopted by my grandmother after her mother died when she was just three years old. To us, she was family. That was the kind of woman my grandmother was—always taking people in, always opening her arms to anyone in need. Everyone in the neighborhood knew her as a second mother. Her heart was big, her arms were open, and her love seemed endless. She was determined, caring, passionate, and strong.

As for me, I had to rise before dawn each morning to do my chores. I didn't enjoy it, but as a child, I had no choice. Saying "no" was not an option as my grandmother was a very strict woman. After completing my chores, I had to prepare for school and make sure I was never late.

I attended Rock Hall Basic School from 1985 to 1990, then moved on to Rock Hall All-Age School, where I graduated in 1998, and later attended Holy Childhood High School. Life at the all-age school was fun when I was there, but once I got home, the fun was over. My close friends then were Karina, Gracy, Olima, Errol, Quendon, Fenton, and the Brown family. Out of them all, Olima and Errol became my best friends.

In Grade 6, we all sat the GSAT exam, but none of us passed. We were crushed. Tears filled our eyes. I cried until my eyes were swollen, not just from disappointment but from fear. I knew my grandmother would not take the news lightly. When I went home, she noticed my red eyes and asked what was wrong. I told her the results were out and that I had failed.

"What are you saying Lavern? That can't be real! Every day I spend my money to send you to school, and this is the result? That's it. No more school for you. It's a waste of time!"

Her words cut deep. I went to my room and stayed there the entire afternoon, silent and withdrawn. The next day, I didn't go to school at all. I stayed home doing chores, but inside, I felt broken. I felt like I no longer belonged, like I wasn't truly part of the family. For the first time, I felt abandoned—like I didn't matter.

LESSONS OF RESILIENCE AND GRATITUDE

Still, I refused to give up. Even in my sadness, I decided to take my books more seriously. I reminded myself that mothers—or in my case, my grandmother—shape lives and inspire dreams. She was strict, but her love was unmatched.

That summer, I asked her if I would be going to summer school. Her reply was firm: *"No. You will stay home for the whole summer."* The summer dragged on, day after day, with the same chores repeated over and over. It was boring and endless. But eventually, summer ended, and Grade 7 began. On that first morning back, I was excited. I couldn't wait to see my friends. When we met, we hugged, laughed, and smiled as if the weight of the world had lifted.

Through all the struggles, I learned something valuable: no matter how stormy life gets, never let it keep you down. Always be thankful and smile because every day God wakes us up is a blessing.

Each morning is a gift, each breath a chance to try again. God is my Father, and I am His child. With Him, every day of life comes with benefits called blessings.

Looking back, I realize that childhood innocence often shields us from the weight of the struggles around us. Even in the midst of limited resources, long walks, and basic living conditions, I found joy in the simple things—playing, laughing, learning, and discovering the world around me.

Those early years remind me that gratitude is not tied to what we have, but to how we see what we have. The truth is, sometimes our greatest blessings are hidden in the places we once wished away. What seemed like hardship then, I now see as preparation.

The little inconveniences—walking in the hot sun, doing without certain comforts, learning discipline early—were actually shaping resilience, humility, and a strong sense of responsibility. These are the same qualities that carry me today.

Life may not always give us ease, but it will always give us lessons. The question is: will we notice them, embrace them, and allow them to build us into who we are meant to be?

REFLECTIONS

1. Hardship Builds Strength

What may seem like suffering in the moment is often the very thing preparing us for resilience later. Early challenges teach discipline, endurance, and responsibility that no comfort could ever offer.

2. The Power of Sacrifice

My grandmother's sacrifices were sometimes harsh, but they were rooted in love. True love is not always soft; sometimes it comes with tough lessons that shape who we become.

3. Education is a Privilege, Not a Guarantee

Even when opportunities seemed slim, the value of education remained clear. Failure is not the end, but an invitation to try again with greater determination.

4. Gratitude in Small Things

Joy is not found in wealth or possessions but in appreciating the little things—friendship, laughter, and God's daily blessings. Gratitude transforms scarcity into abundance.

5. Resilience is a Choice

Though life offered reasons to quit, the decision to keep moving forward was mine. Resilience isn't about never falling—it's about always getting back up.

6. Faith Anchors the Soul

When all else failed, God remained my anchor. He turned pain into preparation and reminded me that every morning is a new chance to rise.

Chapter 2

Lessons In Discipline And Determination

A TIME OF ACHIEVEMENT AND JOY

With all the lessons that I had learnt about the significance of having a good education, I decided to study even harder. Our teacher taught us well, and by the end of the year, I had earned an average of 85%. When my grandmother came to collect my report card, she was overwhelmed with joy. Tears filled her eyes as she hugged me tightly and kissed me on the cheek.

"You've done well, my granddaughter," she said. "I'm very proud of you. From where you were in Grade 6 to where you are now—what a change."

Her words meant the world to me. That summer was one of the best, filled with fun and happiness, because I was allowed to attend summer school. I loved going, especially because all my friends were there.

Lavern Carr

LESSONS IN HUMILITY AND DISCIPLINE

Every day was not perfect. One morning, I was late for class and my teacher, Miss Jones, punished me by making me stand in the corner with a book balanced on my head and my right foot lifted in the air. The entire class burst into laughter, and I felt humiliated. I was so embarrassed that I decided to walk out of the classroom. At first, I wanted to go home, but I quickly realized I couldn't. What would I tell my grandmother? How could I explain being home from school when I wasn't sick?

I decided to stay around the schoolyard until the bell rang for break, then I returned to class and apologized to Miss Jones. She accepted my apology and allowed me back in after lunch. Still, when I walked into the classroom, the students continued laughing at me. I couldn't hold back my tears. I was always shy and easily embarrassed, and this moment cut deep. I sat at my desk with my head down, trying to hide my face.

Miss Jones quickly noticed. "What's so funny?" she asked the class. Silence fell immediately, and she continued her lesson on multiplication. She was a wonderful teacher—strict but fair—and all of us admired her.

That evening, when I got home, my grandmother had already heard about what had happened. She was furious. She scolded me and said, "You must always be early for school! No matter what, make sure you are in class on time. If not, I will beat you every evening." After my flogging, I still had to do my evening chores. I was angry inside, but I dared not let my grandmother see even a trace of it. Growing up with her wasn't easy—she was indeed a disciplinarian. Everything had to be done early and done properly or I would have to do it all over again. But I also knew she wanted the best for me. Like most parents and guardians, she would go to great lengths to prepare me for life.

THE BLESSING OF PRAYER AND GUIDANCE

I still remember one evening after supper when I said I was going to bed. My grandmother came into my room and asked, "Did you say your prayers?" When I said no, she told me to repeat after her:

In my little bed I lie,
Heavenly Father, hear my cry.
Lord, protect me through this night,
And bring me safe to morning light.

From then on, every night before bed, I prayed those words. My grandmother taught me early that being a woman was a blessing, but being a praying woman was a treasure. Women are strong; though life's circumstances may bring us to tears, we still wear beautiful smiles and carry on with grace.

The school years of 1992 to 1994 brought new responsibilities. I was selected as a prefect, which meant I had to set an example for the entire school. Suddenly, there were things I could no longer do; I had to be disciplined, respectful, and consistent. My grandmother was proud—overwhelmed, even—to know I had earned that role. Later, in Grade 9, I was chosen as Deputy Head Girl. My friend, Gracy, was appointed Head Girl, and even though I hadn't gotten the top position, it didn't matter. We worked together as a team and supported each other.

Lavern Carr

GRADUATION, LEADERSHIP, AND NEW BEGINNINGS

Then came the Grade 9 Achievement Exam. I studied hard, and when the results came out, I was overjoyed to see that I had passed with high marks. My grandmother took me to the hairdresser for the very first time to perm my hair for graduation. On graduation day, I was chosen as valedictorian. Shy as I was, I stood before the entire congregation and delivered my speech. Miss Gayle, the principal, congratulated me warmly.

"Well done, Lavern," she said. "I'm proud of you. Keep it up."

For the first time in my life, my grandmother bought me a gift. To others, it might have seemed small, but to me, it was priceless. Tears of joy filled my eyes. Those years, from Grade 7 to Grade 9, I grew into a well-mannered, respectful student. My grandmother always told me, "Manners will take you all over the world." I carried those words with me everywhere I went.

Graduation day was filled with laughter, excitement, and pride. We received our certificates, medals, and encouragement to step boldly into the next chapter of our lives. Soon, it was time to register for high school. I was thrilled when I learned that many of my old friends had also passed for the same school—St. Mary's College. It was a joy for us all to collect our uniforms, timetables, and book lists. The teachers and principal welcomed us warmly, and though we went our separate ways afterward, my friends, Gracy and Olima, smiled and said, "See you next week for summer class."

That summer, we started classes to get familiar with our new school, the teachers, and the students. It was the beginning of an exciting new journey.

REFLECTIONS

1. **Education as a Doorway** – My first experiences with school taught me that education is more than just a building; it is a doorway to new opportunities and possibilities. Every lesson, teacher, and interaction can open paths we never imagined.

2. **Discipline Shapes Character** – Challenges and punishments, though difficult at the time, taught me discipline, resilience, and responsibility. Learning to face consequences prepared me for greater responsibilities in life.

3. **The Power of Prayer and Guidance** – My grandmother's insistence on prayer and moral guidance instilled in me the understanding that inner strength and faith are crucial for overcoming life's obstacles.

4. **Leadership and Teamwork Matter** – Serving as a prefect and, later, Deputy Head Girl showed me the value of leadership, collaboration, and setting a positive example. Success is not just about personal achievement but about uplifting others along the way.

5. **Gratitude and Recognition** – Celebrating achievements, no matter how small, reinforces self-worth and motivates continued effort. My grandmother's pride and support reminded me of the importance of acknowledgment and encouragement.

6. **Vision Beyond Circumstances** – Seeing beyond where I started taught me that our beginnings do not define our endings. With focus and determination, we can rise above limitations and step boldly into our purpose.

7. **The Mind as a Powerful Tool** – Cultivating knowledge and mindset is essential. Education is not only about academics; it is about developing the courage, confidence, and vision to pursue a life of impact and fulfillment.

Chapter 3

A New Horizon: Lessons in Courage and Resilience

The start of a new school year always carried a special kind of excitement. Everyone arrived looking fresh and ready—new shoes polished, uniforms crisp, bags packed with supplies, and hearts full of anticipation. That morning, the entire student body gathered in the assembly hall. The principal welcomed us with warm words, introduced the new teachers, and spoke of the journey ahead. Each department head added their remarks, and the assembly stretched on for more than two hours. Still, no one minded. This was the official beginning of something new, and we all felt it.

When the assembly ended, parents left and students headed to their classrooms. One by one, we stood and introduced ourselves. When I said my name, my teacher smiled mischievously and asked, "Are you sure you're not Shirley from the movie Lover and Shirley?" The whole class erupted in laughter. My cheeks flushed with embarrassment, but I laughed too, realizing it was only a harmless joke.

That first day, we did no real lessons. It was a day for learning faces and spaces. At lunchtime, my friends and I gathered in the cafeteria, sharing bun and cheese, box juices, and laughter. We compared class schedules and talked about which teachers we'd gotten. It wasn't the same as before—Gracy and Olima, my closest friends, weren't in my class anymore. Though we were still at the same school, being apart felt different. I told them I missed them already, and they understood.

When the dismissal bell rang at 3:00 p.m., I hurried out to meet them. Together, we walked to the main road to catch our buses. When I reached home, my grandmother was waiting, as always.

"How was your first day?" she asked.

"It wasn't too bad, Grandma. I like it, and I can't wait to go back tomorrow."

She smiled, touched my forehead gently, and said, "Go change your clothes and do your chores."

LIFE LESSONS BEYOND THE CLASSROOM

Life in the village was simple yet demanding. After chores, I bathed the old-fashioned way—with a pan of water. We didn't have the luxuries of modern bathrooms; we relied on pit toilets and kerosene lamps, or the glow of a full moon when it was bright enough to light the yard. That evening, my dinner was rice and chicken—my favorite. My grandmother was an incredible cook. From simple ingredients, she created flavors that lingered long after the last bite. From the time I was seven, she had been teaching me her skills. "Come here, Lavern," she would call. "See how I wash and season this meat. One day, you'll be the one cooking dinner for me." Her words carried weight beyond the kitchen. "I don't want anyone to take advantage of you when you grow up," she'd say. "So you must learn to cook, wash, clean, and manage life on your own."

DISCOVERING STRENGTH AND RESILIENCE

One afternoon, when I was ten, that training was put to the test. I came home from school to find her weak and unwell.

"Child," she said, "I need some soup, but I can't manage the fire today. Can you make it for me?"

I was nervous, but I nodded. Out in our wood-fire kitchen, I gathered sticks, kerosene oil, and matches. Misra and Patrice- my cousins, watched from a distance as I lit the fire. I washed the pot, filled it with water, and set it to boil. Then I peeled the ground provisions, washed them, and carefully dropped them into the pot. The hot water splashed onto my hand, leaving a blister. I plunged it into cold water and held back tears, remembering my grandmother's words: *"Hold your hand lower when adding food to boiling water."*

I added the seasoning and a packet of cock soup. The dumplings were another story—I kneaded the dough clumsily, and it stuck all over my hands. Frustrated, I tossed the dough away, deciding there would be no dumplings in this soup. Still, I carried on. When the soup was done, I brought a bowl to my grandmother. She sipped carefully, then smiled. "Not bad, my child. This soup could save a life." That evening, everyone ate and ate until their bellies were full. To my surprise, the next day, my grandmother told her friends about it. "Would you believe my granddaughter boiled the sweetest soup?" she said, with pride filling her voice. I listened quietly with my heart swelling. I was only ten, but in that moment, I realized something important: I was capable. I could be trusted. And though my soup had no dumplings, it carried the taste of effort, resilience, and love.

REFLECTIONS

1. Life will often place responsibilities on us before we feel ready, but it is in those very moments that hidden strength is revealed.

2. Courage is not the absence of fear, but the choice to act despite it. Even small actions, like making a simple soup, can carry profound lessons of resilience.

3. We often discover our true capabilities when we are tested. Challenges reveal that we are far more capable than we first believe.

4. The lessons passed down by those who came before us are not just about skills, but about survival, independence, and wisdom for life.

5. Resilience means stepping forward with faith and determination, even when uncertainty and fear are present.

Chapter 4

Lessons in Life, Loss, and Love

MORNING STRENGTH AND DAILY RESILIENCE

Most mornings, I felt as though an angel whispered blessings into my day—filling my basket with joy, peace, love, strength, grace, and hope for all humankind. I've come to realize that health does not always come from medicine; most of the time it flows from peace of mind, a heart at rest, laughter, and love. I often remind myself: *I am here to succeed, designed to win, equipped to overcome, anointed to prosper, and blessed to be a blessing.* I decided to let go of yesterday's hurts and hold on to the love that carried me through each day.

Grandma was feeling much better and was grateful that I had prepared a meal for her the evening before. When I asked if I could go to school, she said, "I would never stop you from school, Lavern. Go and get ready." I felt relieved—school was my escape, my light, my joy. I got dressed, feeling elegant in my simple uniform, and met my friends at the bus stop. That morning, transportation never came, so we walked nearly 19 kilometers to school. It was long and tiring, but we laughed, shared stories, and made the best of it. We arrived late, bodies hot and sweaty, but the walk gave us strength in ways we couldn't see then. After school, we chose to walk home again, saving our bus fare to buy a small meal from Miss Carol, who sold cooked food by the roadside.

FACING LOSS AND LIFE'S FRAGILITY

That evening, when I reached home, Grandma called me to sit. Her face was serious.

She said, "Lavern, your friend Quendon…he died."

I froze. "Who, Grandma?"

"Quendon," she repeated.

Tears streamed down my face as grief pierced me. He had gone swimming at Hellshire with friends and never came back. His body was found the next morning, washed ashore. The news shattered me. Quendon was kind, full of life, and loved by many. His loss left an emptiness that words could not fill.

The community mourned deeply. At the "night night," all of his friends gathered. It was bittersweet—though grief was heavy, being together gave us comfort. The following week at his burial, the church overflowed with weeping and mourning. Yet, I felt grateful he was given a service that honored his short but meaningful life. To this day, Quendon remains in my heart, a reminder of how fragile and precious life is.

If you've ever lost someone you loved, you know the ache that words can barely touch. It's a kind of pain that lingers in the quiet moments—the empty chair, the phone call that will never come, the laughter that now only lives in memory. Grief has a way of stopping time, leaving you standing in the middle of life's road with no clear direction, just a heart heavy with what was and what will never be again. And yet, in that weight, there is also proof: you grieve deeply because you loved deeply.

The journey through loss is never easy. Some days you may feel strong, almost whole, and other days the wave of sorrow may knock you down without warning. You may even wonder if you'll ever feel "normal" again. But hear this—grief does not mean you are broken; it means you are human. It means you dared to love, to open your heart wide, to let someone in so fully that their absence feels like a wound. That kind of love is rare, and though it hurts, it is also holy.

If you are walking through that valley right now, know this: healing does not come by forgetting, but by remembering differently. The moments you shared—their voice, their touch, the way they made you laugh—these are treasures time cannot steal. Instead of focusing on the last goodbye, hold on to the countless hellos, the small joys, the lessons, the love. Their legacy is alive in you, in how you live, how you love, and how you choose to keep going, even when it hurts.

One day, the tears will not sting as sharply. The memories will bring more smiles than pain. And when you take a step forward, it won't mean you are leaving them behind—it means you are carrying them with you. Love never dies; it simply changes form. Perhaps the most powerful way to honor someone you've lost is to live in a way that reflects the love they gave you—to shine brighter, love harder, and give freely, knowing that their presence has forever shaped who you are.

SURVIVAL, GRATITUDE, AND TRUE HAPPINESS

Soon after, I began high school at St. Mary's College. The early days were filled with excitement and pride, but reality shifted quickly. There were mornings when Grandma could not give me lunch money. She was under pressure, carrying not only me but her own children and the others she had taken in. Yet she never turned anyone away. That was her way—her arms and her heart were always open.

I remember walking to school with my friends, confessing that I had no lunch money. Gracy and Olima smiled and said, "Lavern, don't worry. We are all friends. Everything will be okay." That reassurance warmed my heart.

Even on hungry days, I pressed on. We would sit under mango and orange trees, climbing and laughing, finding joy in small things. But joy was sometimes shadowed by fear. Once, after climbing trees, I stained my only school uniform. I cried, terrified Grandma would be angry, for we couldn't afford another. That evening, she didn't notice, and I quickly washed it—relieved, yet reminded of how delicate life was.

Grandma's words became my compass: "Life is sometimes salt, sometimes sugar. Focus on your blessings, not your misfortunes. Be grateful for what you have, and one day, things will be better."

There were also strange moments—like the morning I found white powder in my shoes. Grandma quickly squeezed lime over them, warning me not to wear them. Instead, she gave me borrowed slippers and tied my toe to make it look like I was injured. For weeks, I wore them to school, embarrassed but grateful when her husband, Mr. Stewart, the shoemaker, eventually made me new shoes. He saved me from shame, and I thanked him over and over.

Through it all, Grandma's love anchored me. She was strict, sometimes painfully so, but I understood—it was her way of molding me for survival. Even when life felt unfair, even when the hardship of life left me in tears, I knew she wanted only the best for me.

Later, I had the opportunity to live with Auntie Loveline on Molynes Road. Her home felt like a palace compared to what I knew. I had my own room, my own bathroom, even a television. I felt like a queen. She gave me bus fare and lunch money, and I started saving in a piggy bank. However, her ways were peculiar—she insisted I iron only one uniform and take the rest to my grandma for pressing. At first, I laughed it off, but soon I grew weary. Material comfort without peace was not worth the cost, so I chose to return to Grandma. I learned then that life is not about vanity or appearances. True happiness cannot be bought with money or fine things—it comes from love, peace, and purpose.

REFLECTIONS

1. Life is fragile, and tomorrow is never promised—losing Quendon reminded me of the preciousness of every moment.

2. Determination and resilience are built through perseverance, even in hardships, such as walking long distances to school.

3. True wealth is not found in material possessions but in love, relationships, and supportive communities.

4. Strength is developed in the shadows of lack—wearing slippers to school, a single uniform, and hunger pains teach endurance.

5. Life's "salt and sugar" moments teach balance: hardships are temporary, but the lessons they leave are eternal.

6. Love, discipline, and guidance from elders shape character and prepare one for survival and future challenges.

Chapter 5

Trials, Trust, and Lessons in Provision

CHOOSING MY PATH AMIDST FINANCIAL HURDLES

Fifth form marked the threshold of a new chapter in my life. I had carefully selected my subjects—Mathematics, English, Computer Science, Integrated Science, Biology, and Principles of Business. These were not chosen lightly; each one reflected both my ability and my determination to pass the Caribbean Examinations Council (CXC) exams. For the first time, I felt a sense of empowerment in shaping my own academic destiny.

I hurried home with the good news, excited to share it with my grandmother. She listened with pride in her eyes, but sorrow lingered in her voice. The registration fee for all six subjects amounted to 3,350 Jamaican dollars—money she simply did not have. My heart sank, yet I refused to let despair win. For the first time in my life, I resolved to ask my father for help.

The following day, I stopped at his house after school. With trembling hands, I showed him the registration slip. His reply startled me: "I don't have any money now, but come back four days before the due date. I'll give it to you then." I left his house glowing.

For the first time, my father had promised to do something for me. My heart swelled with pride; I smiled the entire evening, so much so that everyone in the house noticed. When I told my grandmother, she raised her eyebrows, unconvinced. "Let's see, my child, how it will go." But I clung to hope, cherishing the thought that my father might finally come through for me.

DISAPPOINTMENT AND FINDING SMALL BLESSINGS

Two weeks later, my mother visited. I eagerly told her about my father's promise, expecting her to share in my joy. Instead, she sighed and said, "Your father will not give you that money. Find another way." Her words crushed me. Tears welled up, for I had no other source. When the payment deadline drew near, I returned to my father's house. He wasn't home. I waited for more than two hours, only to be told by his wife, Margaret, that I should go home. Disappointment cut through me like a knife. I wept bitterly to my grandmother, asking, "What do I do now?"

She held me close and said softly, "You can imagine how beautiful heaven must be. It is not only for the rich, but also for the poor. God's light is always shining, and I know you will walk through that light. This burden will soon lift from you. Be patient—everything will be okay."

The next morning, I shared my sorrow with my cousin, Greg. His eyes softened, and he said, "Don't worry, I can pay for two subjects. I don't have enough for all, but at least you can take some." I leapt for joy, tears streaming down my face—grateful for even a partial blessing. With his help, I registered for two subjects.

I was happy, but the weight of disappointment clung to me. During exams, my mind was clouded. I earned two grade threes, when I knew I was capable of grade ones. Because I did not have the required five subjects, I was unable to graduate from St. Mary's College. The shame of watching my peers in gowns while I stood empty-handed left me devastated. Yet I refused to let this failure define me. I reminded myself: my education does not end here. At the Catholic Church I attended, the sisters who supported us encouraged me. I sought their help to repeat the fifth form at Holy Childhood High. I completed the forms and requirements, but could not pay the fees. Once again, lack of money stood between me and my dreams.

DESPERATION AND THE LESSONS OF TRUST

At age fourteen, I met a guy by the name of Nathaniel. He came into my life like a blessing, almost as if God had sent him as a support system. He offered financial help without ever making advances, often reminding me that he simply admired my dedication to school and the person I was becoming. He helped with my books and uniform, and over time, we became close friends. He even threw me a wonderful birthday party, and Grandma grew curious about where it all came from. When she met Nathaniel, she quickly expressed her dislike and warned me that he would eventually hurt me. I assured her we were just friends, choosing to believe Nathaniel's words that his support came with no strings attached. To me, he seemed like an angel sent from above, and despite Grandma's concerns, Nathaniel and I remained friends. Deep down, I thought that Grandma didn't have a clue what she was talking about. I told Nathaniel, and he wanted us to keep our friendship a secret. I thought, given that I no longer had to worry about my school fees and books, this was the best thing to do.

I continued to work hard in school and remained focused on my studies. I would ensure that my homework was completed and I was fully ready for school the following day. Nathaniel continued to offer the financial support that I needed, and that season was not that stressful for my grandmother. Four years later, Nathaniel told me that we could go out for dinner on my 18th birthday if I gave him a chance. I really didn't have an issue with that, given that he was such a strong support system for me.

REFLECTIONS

1. Disappointment can be painful, especially when those you rely on fail to deliver, but it teaches resilience and dependence on God.

2. Small acts of help, like my cousin Greg's, show that blessings often come from unexpected sources.

3. Poverty robs you of future opportunities. Make a decision early to break poverty from your life. When my father was a "no show" to pay my school fees, it showed me that I needed to work hard to capture every opportunity in life.

4. True provision must bring peace; material support that robs one of peace is not a blessing but a burden.

5. Determination and hope can sustain you through repeated obstacles and setbacks.

6. Discernment is vital—learning to distinguish between temporary relief and long-term safety is a key life skill.

Chapter 6

Foundations, Loss, and Reclaiming My Future

When the new school year approached, I had everything a student could hope for: a new uniform, books, a bag, socks, and shoes. Nathaniel had provided it all. He even asked about my school fees, and when I admitted I had no idea how they would be paid, he said, "Don't worry, I'll handle it."

The very next day, Nathaniel drove me to school and paid the fees in full. I was stunned, overwhelmed, and speechless. Deep down, I felt relief—everything I needed to return to school had been provided. On September 3, 1998, I walked into school with pride. Yet beneath the excitement was the secret I carried: I was still depending on Nathaniel, and I could not let Grandma know. She might have suspected, but I never confessed.

THE END OF CHILDHOOD AND A FIRM ROOF

On my eighteenth birthday, Nathaniel took me out to supper. It was the first time in my life I had celebrated in such a way. I did not return until the next morning. My grandmother was waiting at the door. Her eyes told me she had not slept all night.

"Where are you coming from, Lavern?" she asked. Twice. I said nothing. She reached for her belt as she always did when she was displeased. But this time, I grabbed the strap and said, "Grandma, I turned eighteen yesterday. Don't you think I'm a woman now? Isn't it time to put down the belt?"

Her reply cut deep: "As long as you live under my roof, you will live by my rules. If you don't like them, you can pack your bags and leave."

That was January 1, 1999—the day childhood ended in my grandmother's house.

THE FRAGILITY OF DEPENDENCE

Despite her disapproval, I continued seeing Nathaniel. He treated me like royalty, provided everything I needed, and showed me a world beyond my village. With Nathaniel, I never lacked. For over four years, we were inseparable.

One evening, I got the shock of my life! Nathaniel called and told me it was over. He was migrating with his family. His last words were: "Remember, I will always love you." That was the end. No more visits. No more calls. Just silence.

His absence hit me like a storm. Not only had I lost someone I had come to love, but also the only source I had to pay my CXC fees. Once again, I was standing at the edge of opportunity with empty hands. My grandmother could barely find food for us, let alone cover exam costs. I pleaded with the sisters at school, but it was too late—submissions for exam entries had closed. Frustrated and humiliated, I stopped attending classes. Nothing made sense anymore. I felt stupid, stuck, and abandoned all over again. So I left Holy Childhood High. If education seemed out of reach, I decided I would find work instead.

NEW OPPORTUNITIES AND THE POWER OF SELF-RELIANCE

My siblings became my anchor. My brother and my only sister, Simone, depended on me. They were my heart, my pride, my reason to press forward. So I took a job at a bleach factory on Ken Hill Drive. It wasn't what I wanted, but family came first.

During that time, I met a friend, Nadine, who told me about a government-sponsored HEART program in Early Childhood Education. There were no tuition fees—just the cost of supplies. It felt like a miracle. I applied, was accepted, and began classes in September 1999. For the first time, I didn't have to worry about how to pay.

The program required us to prepare lesson charts, teach young children, and complete both practical and theory exams. I threw myself into the work, grateful for another chance at education. At the end, I passed my exams and earned my first official certificate. That certificate was more than paper—it was proof that my story wasn't finished.

My journey continued at Calabar High School in Kingston, where I studied Mathematics and Civics. I passed both. For the first time, I felt momentum building again. I was not only rebuilding my life but also creating a foundation to take care of my siblings and move us forward.

REFLECTIONS

1. Depending on others can provide temporary comfort, but cannot guarantee long-term security.

2. Love without responsibility or boundaries can be dangerous and misleading.

3. The closure of one door often opens another—new opportunities can emerge when old supports disappear.

4. Self-reliance is the ultimate freedom; when you stand on your own, no one can take that ground from you.

5. Family responsibilities can be a source of motivation and a reminder to keep moving forward despite setbacks.

6. Education may come in unexpected forms, but embracing every opportunity is crucial for growth and stability.

Chapter 7

A Key of My Own

UNLOCKING MY FIRST SANCTUARY

There are certain milestones in life that seem small to the outside world but mean everything to the one living them. For me, one of those moments was when my grandmother gave me a room that once belonged to my mother. My uncle, Donovan, had originally given it to her, but since she was not around, Grandma passed it on to me and my siblings.

The room was in no condition to be called a home—it needed repairs, especially the ceiling, which gaped open to the sky. Yet, I saw not what it was, but what it could be. I saved what I could, bought materials, and fixed it up so that when we lay down at night, the stars would not peer in uninvited. For the first time in my life, I held a key that opened a door of my own. I did not have to call out for permission to enter. I had a place to lock, a space to belong, and within that modest room, I found a freedom deeper than walls could hold.

My siblings shared in that joy. My sister, Simone, disciplined and dedicated, went off to Tarrant High School with pride, while my younger brother, Ramon, attended Rock Hall. Simone approached school with determination; each day, she would recount her lessons with enthusiasm. Ramon, however, resisted. He lacked focus, and often it seemed that school could not hold his attention. I tried to step into the role of both mother and father, guiding him as best as I could, determined that his story would not be written by neglect.

REJECTION AND THE ROAD TO INDEPENDENCE

Life, as always, tested me.

One day, I returned home to find Simone crying. She told me that my aunt had struck her after she had cooked, accusing her of not leaving enough food. When I confronted her, words turned sharp, and emotions flared. Tools were drawn and, in the chaos, my aunt got hurt. The police were called, and for a moment, I thought that represented the end for me. My grandmother intervened, assuring the officers she would deal with the matter at home. Yet that evening, I was told to leave—that I was no longer welcome in what I still considered my rightful place. I refused. That room was my mother's legacy to me. Still, the rejection stung deeply. The following day, after pushing myself through work despite not feeling well, I returned to find my belongings thrown outside in the rain. Simone was standing beneath the shed, helpless and hurt. My heart sank. With nowhere to go, we sought refuge at my cousin Katherine's house for the night. Tears flowed endlessly as I wrestled with the question: *Where will we go? What will become of us now?*

A NEW HOME, A NEW BEGINNING

Katherine told me about a man named Mr. River who had rooms for rent. I wasted no time. The next morning, I found him, explained my situation, and to my relief, he told me a two-bedroom was available immediately. I cleaned it that evening, and with the help of my siblings and a friend, we moved in.

That night, tears of sorrow turned into tears of joy. For the first time in a long time, my siblings and I felt safe, sheltered, and free. Months later, I received a call that Grandma was unwell. I went to see her and found her weak, her spirit subdued. She confessed her love for me, assuring me that much of what had happened was not her decision but the will of my aunt. Her words softened me, but I also asked her why she allowed her children to dictate her household. She said little, and I left, promising to return the next day.

When I did, I carried soup for her. She sat outside on a water tank, frail but grateful, and blessed me with words that pierced my heart: "May your basket never go empty. God bless you." I smiled, humbled by her blessing. Moments later, one of my aunts—the very one who had once thrown my belongings into the rain—asked if she could share the soup. I handed it over silently, reflecting on the strange twists of life. Indeed, life is full of surprises. One day you are cast out, the next you are asked to give. Somehow, giving always becomes its own form of victory.

REFLECTIONS

1. Possession of a key is more than access—it is ownership of your destiny. A small room with a repaired ceiling taught me the meaning of freedom.

2. Family can wound, but family can also bless. The same household that rejected me also gave me words of blessing that I carry to this day.

3. When you are pushed out, do not despair—often it is God's way of pushing you into purpose.

4. The cycle of giving never ends. Even those who hurt you may one day need your kindness. Choosing to give, even then, is the highest form of strength.

Chapter 8

Love, Loss, and Lessons in Truth

After unsuccessful attempts to find work in the early childhood field, I turned my focus elsewhere and landed in the most unexpected place—a bar. Through an acquaintance named Dwayne, I was introduced to his friend, who owned a local establishment. Though I had no experience, I pleaded with him for a chance. I even offered to work one week without pay, shadowing my cousin, Katherine, who was already employed there. He agreed, and by the next day, I reported for duty—early, eager, and determined. Within just two days, I had learned the ropes. It wasn't just a job to me; it was survival. Dwayne began stopping by frequently. He checked on me, spoke kindly, and soon we exchanged numbers. Though handsome and charming, I reminded myself that I was focused on my career, not romance. But eventually, through his persistence, our friendship grew deeper.

A CAR, A CHOICE, AND A COSTLY MISTAKE

During this time, my aunt offered to sell me her damaged Charade. With Dwayne's encouragement, I purchased it for 40,000 Jamaican dollars, plus an additional $30,000 for parts and repairs. I paid my aunt in full, hired a mechanic, and soon had my very first car.

Unfortunately, the joy of ownership was short-lived. One Sunday, while cooking at home, we ran out of gas. Though the car wasn't yet licensed or insured, Dwayne and I took the risk of driving to buy fuel. On Cooper's Hill, we were pulled over. The officers demanded documentation that I did not have. Despite my pleas, I was ticketed heavily—over 40,000 Jamaican dollars. I spoke with one of the senior officers on location, and we were able to work out a deal. That deal cost me $25,000. I had little choice; it was either that or pay a ticket of over $40,000. That money was my only savings for emergencies. Handing it over broke me. I wept the entire night, making sandwiches for my siblings instead of finishing dinner. It was a moment of both shame and survival.

A LOVE THAT WAS DECEPTION

Through it all, Dwayne remained supportive, caring not just for me but for my siblings as well. He moved in with us, and for a time, I believed I had found a partner I could trust. He encouraged me, helped carry our burdens, and gave me hope.

But the truth shattered everything. One evening, my grandmother revealed that Dwayne was married with three children. At first, I refused to believe her, dismissing it as another judgment, but when I confronted Dwayne, he admitted it. My heart broke. The man I loved deeply had betrayed me with silence and lies. I told him it was over. Love, I realized, is not supposed to hurt—it is supposed to honor. To love someone is to protect, not deceive. Though I ended the relationship, the bond we shared as friends endured.

The truth hit harder when Dwayne's wife confronted me directly. She had heard about our relationship, and when she came to me with her pain, I could see her desperation, not just as a wife, but as a mother longing for her children to have their father back. I assured her that my relationship with Dwayne was over. To my surprise, she later brought their children to meet me. They were beautiful, full of innocence, and I immediately admired them. I encouraged her never to give up on her family and told her I was sorry for the role I unknowingly played in her hurt. Dwayne stood there, unable to look me in the eye. But I released him, forgave him, and chose peace. In time, I realized that while his deception cut deep, the lessons it taught me were invaluable.

CHOOSING MYSELF AGAIN

Even after all the turmoil, I carried no bitterness. Dwayne returned to his family, and though our paths still crossed at the bar, my heart had shifted. I loved him still, but in a different way—no longer as a partner, but as a person I prayed would become the man his family needed. In the midst of heartbreak, I made myself a promise: I would move on, grow stronger, and never again compromise my worth for temporary comfort. This chapter closed with both pain and freedom, but most importantly, with wisdom.

REFLECTIONS

1. **Persistence Opens Doors** – Even when inexperienced, determination and humility can create opportunities where none seem to exist.

2. **Choices Have Consequences** – Taking shortcuts or risks (like driving without documents) can cost dearly, teaching us to value wisdom over haste.

3. **Love Without Truth is a Lie** – Real love is built on honesty. Without it, affection becomes deception, and trust cannot survive.

4. **Forgiveness Heals the Heart** – Releasing anger toward those who hurt you is not weakness; it is strength that allows you to grow.

5. **Self-Worth is Non-Negotiable** – When you know who you are and what you deserve, you refuse to settle for relationships or situations that dishonor you.

Chapter 9

Love, Responsibility, and the Unseen Hand of Grace

A LIGHT WALKS INTO MY LIFE

I was working in the sales department at 2B Ken Hill Drive in Pembroke Hall, where I cashed and served customers. One day, a Rastaman came in to buy five gallons of armoural and five gallons of bleach. I went out from behind the counter to serve him, partly out of duty, but also out of curiosity. His clothes were spotless white, his teeth gleamed as bright as his attire, and there was something about his presence that demanded a second glance.

When he left, I whispered to my coworkers, "That Rastaman looks too good to ignore." Two weeks later, he returned for the same products. I offered him the old sale price as a gesture of goodwill, since he was clearly a loyal customer. That day, he asked for my phone number. I resisted at first, joking that I didn't have a phone, but he didn't buy my excuse. "What's your name?" he pressed.

"Look at your receipt," I replied with a smile.

"Donald," he said.

"That's a lovely name, Donald. Have a good day, sir."

For five months, Donald kept coming to the store, faithfully, until I finally gave him both my home and cell numbers. That very night, he called, his voice steady, his tone respectful. He asked about my life and my siblings. I explained that I had left a relationship built on lies, and I was not interested in stepping into heartbreak again. His reply was simple: *"A beautiful girl like you deserves better."*

At first, I resisted his flattery. But in time, I began to sense something different about him—a kindness, a sincerity. He made it clear that if he loved me, he would also love and accept my siblings. That alone softened my heart.

LOVE THAT CAME WITH ROSES

Donald was consistent. He called me every night and soon invited me to his home. I still remember the first time I went—dressed in a full red suit, nervous under the stares of neighbors. He reassured me, "Don't worry, they're just curious." So, in the comfort of his home, our conversations stretched into the night, flowing easily as if we had known each other for years.

Over time, Donald began to show me what genuine care looked like. He was never careless with my trust. One Friday evening, when he arrived late to pick me up, he knocked on my door with a bunch of fresh red roses, apologizing for the delay. I blushed, realizing that this man's love was not just words—it was thoughtful action.

He introduced me to his parents as well as his sisters. From the first moment, they welcomed me as if I belonged. His mother was jovial but firm, his father calm and collected. I cooked breakfast for them one Saturday morning, and in that simple act, I felt as though I had already become part of their family. Donald's love was very caring. On one rainy day, when hunger gnawed at me, he went out into the storm—hail and all—just to buy me a bun and cheese. That kind of love can't be fabricated. It was real, sacrificial, and pure.

FAMILY TRIALS AND UNSHAKEN FAITH

But love stories rarely unfold without challenges. My younger sister, only seventeen at the time, was dating a boy named Marlon in Red Hills. Tragedy struck one evening when Marlon was shot—eight bullets meant for someone else tore into his body. My brother risked his life to pull him from the bushes, while a taxi driver, the only one brave enough to help, rushed us down the hill. Donald and my brother carried Marlon into our van, and we drove him to the University of the West Indies hospital.

I prayed desperately that night: *"Lord, have mercy, let this young man live."* Marlon survived but lay broken, strapped with tubes, barely able to move. For five long months, my sister stood faithfully by his side. What I didn't know at first was that she was carrying his child.

I was torn—upset that I hadn't been more vigilant as her older sister, yet deeply proud of her courage. When she finally gave birth to a beautiful baby boy, Romain, my heart melted. From the moment he smiled at me, I vowed that nothing in this world would keep me from protecting him.

In the midst of all this, Donald stepped in like a father figure, not only to me but also to my siblings. He took my brother under his wing, teaching him life lessons, guiding him with patience and wisdom. Their bond grew so strong that people often thought they were twins. Through the storms, through heartbreak and uncertainty, Donald became more than a partner. He became a safe place, a provider, and an anchor for my family.

FLASHBACK – THE CAR THAT STOLE MY PEACE

Even as life with Donald brought love and stability, there was still one matter that lingered in the background like an unfinished chapter: the car I had purchased from my aunt. Years had passed, yet I still had no papers for the vehicle. Time and again, I went to my grandmother for help, asking her to speak with her daughter—my aunt—about the documents. Each time, I was told to wait. What was supposed to be my first step into independence became a chain around my ankle. The car, fixed and ready, sat useless in the garage. Without insurance, fitness, or a license, it was a trap waiting to happen, and I was unwilling to fall into another police incident like before.

My frustration grew. How could my own aunt, who had taken my money in full, withhold what was rightfully mine? My uncle himself asked, *"How could she do this to her own niece?"* It was becoming clear that my aunt had either lost the papers or perhaps never had them. I started to believe my grandmother and aunt had steered me into the wrong choice all along.

I remembered the accident when Denton, my aunt's spouse, had crashed the car in Mount Zion. He didn't survive, and I began to wonder if the documents had disappeared in that chaos—or if there was a deeper dishonesty at play. After Denton's funeral, I waited two months before pressing again for the papers. The response was the same: *"Wait."* But how long should someone wait for justice?

Eventually, I decided to let the car go. I handed it over to my cousin, hoping he could make use of it. But Donald, ever practical, challenged me: "Why not let someone run it as a taxi? You spent too much to just give it away." At his encouragement, I struck a deal with his friend. The risk was great—the car had no papers, and if the police caught him, the consequences could be severe. But Andre was willing, and soon enough, the car was back on the road, finally earning money.

It wasn't long before trouble found us again. His friend was chased by a police officer one afternoon; he barely managed to escape and hide the vehicle. Shaken, he decided he would not drive it again. I then gave it to my cousin, who worked on it for a while until it finally broke down, and he sold the parts. In the end, the car that was supposed to represent my freedom became nothing but frustration. I learned a painful truth: not every opportunity that looks like a blessing truly is. Sometimes, even family can mislead you, and sometimes letting go is the only way forward.

REFLECTIONS

1. **Love is more than attraction**—it is shown in daily sacrifices, like buying a bun in the rain or extending kindness to your family.

2. **Family challenges test the strength of relationships**—true love endures not only romance but also the weight of real-life responsibilities.

3. **God often sends people at the right time**—Donald's presence was not accidental; he was a blessing sent to help carry the load.

4. **Trials refine our character**—my sister's situation with Marlon taught me that even in the hardest times, faith and courage can sustain us.

5. **Every hardship carries hidden grace**—though pain came, so did unexpected joy, like the gift of my nephew's smile and the steady hand of love in my life.

6. **Some investments are lessons, not returns**—that car taught me more about trust and discernment than it ever did about transportation.

7. **God can use disappointment to redirect us**—when one door closes, it is often because He has a better one waiting.

8. **Letting go brings peace**—some burdens must be released so you can walk freely into your true destiny.

Chapter 10

Driving Through Fear - Roads That Shape Us

After dating Donald for more than five years, I decided it was time to return to school. I enrolled at HEART Trust, where I completed a one-year course in Food Service and earned a certificate. Despite this, I was unable to secure a job in that field. Determined not to give up, I applied to the Jamaica Urban Transit Company. Within months, I received a call for an interview, and soon after, I was training for what would become a life-changing career.

My trainers believed in me from the beginning. On my very first day on the road, I was praised as "the best and most outstanding driver." Out of 22 drivers—20 of them men and only 2 women—I was recognized as the best. It was a proud moment, a reminder that perseverance pays off.

LEARNING THE ROADS, LEARNING MYSELF

Soon after, JUTC assigned me to route training. My first was the 81 to Wellington Town, then 86 through South Camp Road, along with several others. Over the course of three months, I mastered these routes and began carrying passengers regularly. The job was often exhausting, especially driving buses without air conditioning under the hot sun, but I pressed on. My prayer was simple: *one day, I hoped to drive a newer bus with AC.* That prayer was answered when my supervisor asked if I knew the Port Royal route. My "yes" led to my first opportunity to drive a cooler, modern bus—a blessing I didn't take lightly.

When my probation ended, I officially became a full-time driver. Compliments from passengers flowed regularly: *"Driver, you're beautiful and you can really handle that bus—keep up the good work."* Their words encouraged me to keep pressing forward. I built lasting friendships, including one with Miss Monice, who took me in like family. Every Sunday, she prepared fish for me, ensuring I had a warm meal, even when I worked late. In Port Royal, I was deeply respected and protected; no one dared to disrespect me, knowing the community would defend me. However, the job also carried risks. One night, I was sent to August Town at 9:30 p.m., only to learn that another driver had been robbed and killed earlier on the same route. Fear gripped me, but I drove straight back to the depot without stopping for passengers. That night, I realized just how dangerous the work was. Each day on the road was a test of faith, reminding me to cover myself in prayer and rely on God's protection.

TRIALS, DANGERS, AND THE HAND OF GOD

Eventually, the company reassigned me from the Port Royal route to the hills. The roads there were rough, filled with gullies and sharp turns. While other female drivers hesitated, I accepted the challenge. Driving those routes strengthened my courage and confidence until I knew I could handle any large vehicle, anywhere in the world. My passengers on routes 52 and 53 grew to love me just as much as those from Port Royal had, and I gained a reputation as a driver who could be trusted under pressure.

There I was, carrying out my daily duties, when danger found me again. One afternoon, while picking up a passenger, a man boarded my bus, pointed a gun at me, and demanded the government's money. I didn't hesitate—I threw the money toward him and shut the door. The passengers shouted for me to drive to the nearest police station, but all I could think was, *"He could have pulled the trigger."* By the grace of God, he didn't.

I filed a report at the police station and later with my manager, but the experience left me shaken. For three days, I couldn't bring myself to work. During that time, I reflected deeply. God had spared me. That man could have ended my life, but mercy spoke on my behalf. I realized then that no one walks the road of success without first passing through streets of fear, failure, or uncertainty. God never promised us an easy journey, but He did promise a purposeful destination.

Even in my loneliness, I felt God beside me. *"I walk with the Lord when my heart needs company, and I hold His hand when I feel all alone. When I need someone to lean on, He is the only one I can always rely on."* Each morning, I whispered a prayer: *"Lord, I step into today with faith. No matter how hard yesterday was, I know Your mercies are new today."* Those words carried me through the darkest moments on the road.

Life often takes us on roads we never expected, but sometimes those very roads prepare us for courage, resilience, and faith. My journey with the Jamaica Urban Transit Company (JUTC) was not just about learning to drive buses—it was about learning to trust God, to trust myself, and to embrace challenges as stepping stones toward purpose.

REFLECTIONS

1. Faithful beginnings create strong foundations. Even when others doubt your abilities, staying true to your calling and putting in the work will eventually silence the doubts.

2. Excellence shines, even in adversity. Being one of only two women among many men, yet standing out as the best, shows that true dedication and skill cannot be hidden.

3. Trust is essential in relationships. Without trust, love weakens. Support should come with belief, not suspicion.

4. Courage is refined through trials. Every dangerous road, every robbery faced, and every long night built inner resilience and proved that fear does not define destiny.

5. Community is a shield of love. The Port Royal residents who defended and protected me reminded me that genuine kindness always finds its way back to you.

6. Every setback is an unseen setup. Even the frightening moments, like being robbed, revealed that God's hand was covering me.

7. Faith is the compass for survival. The journey was never easy, but trusting God through each roadblock gave peace and the courage to press forward.

8. Success requires perseverance. Driving dangerous routes, enduring hard conditions, and still excelling taught me that miracles blossom when you refuse to quit.

Chapter 11

Loss, Resilience, and the Power of Inner Strength

MOMENTS OF BEAUTY AMIDST LIFE'S STORMS

Life often unfolds as a delicate balance between joy and sorrow, between moments of peace and seasons of grief. My years at JUTC opened the door for new opportunities, including a well-deserved vacation, but they also introduced me to some of my most painful experiences of loss.

After working diligently for more than two years, I finally received vacation leave and traveled to Barbados. It was my first time leaving Jamaica, and the experience felt like stepping into another world. The island was small yet breathtakingly beautiful—you could drive around it in a single day. The beaches shimmered like jewels under the sun, and the hospitality of the people warmed my spirit.

Unlike the stories I had heard of visitors facing hardships at immigration, our welcome was smooth and respectful. I didn't miss Jamaica for a moment. Barbados was filled with joy, reflection, and a sense of calm that refreshed my soul. I learned something during that trip—self-control is strength, and calmness is mastery. I realized that one must arrive at a place where moods are no longer dictated by the actions of others, and where emotions do not overpower intelligence.

On returning to Jamaica, I received devastating news: Daniel's mother had been diagnosed with breast cancer. To me, she was more than his mother; she was mine too. She shared her wisdom, confided in me, and cared for me as though I had been born to her.

When she went for surgery, her health began to decline, yet she continued caring for those around her. Her passing shattered our hearts. The community mourned her deeply, and her legacy of love and faith left a permanent mark on my spirit.

At the same time, challenges at work arose. I had been nominated for training to drive larger buses—a promotion that would have advanced my career—but my manager dismissed me, claiming I was too young. Rejection became a teacher, fueling my determination to prove my capabilities.

GRIEF, JUSTICE, AND THE STRENGTH WITHIN

While working at JUTC, I faced one of the darkest moments of my life. My cousin, Everton, a humble and respectable young man, was wrongfully accused of being the leader of a gang. As far as I knew, my cousin was a devoted father and a supportive cousin, the kind who would wash and iron my uniforms for the week, cook meals with me, and share in the little joys of life. Whatever I had, I would share with him, and he, in turn, gave me unwavering kindness.

The Struggle is Real

One day, while I was on duty, I received a devastating call—there had been gunshots at my home, and Everton was dead. My heart sank. I immediately left the unit I was driving and went to my supervisor to tell him I could not continue. This was an emergency that tore through every fiber of my being. When I arrived at my home, I was met by a barricade of police officers at the gate, refusing to let us enter. Then, with my own eyes, I watched as they dragged my cousin's body from the house and threw him into the back of a police vehicle. The image is one that has never left me.

Eventually, they allowed me inside, and what I saw was beyond words. My house was in complete disarray—clothes scattered everywhere, everything overturned, and the washroom covered in blood. I could see the desperate trail of his final moments: how he tried to escape through the grilled window after the first shot, but there was no way out. When I confronted one of the officers and asked what had happened, he claimed there had been a shootout between my cousin and the police. But I knew, deep within my spirit, that it was not true. My cousin did not own a gun. He had already decided to put down the lifestyle of the past and focus on raising his daughter, choosing instead to live a simple, honest life.

Through my tears, I told the officers what weighed heavily on my heart: *"You have families, you have children of your own. You are meant to protect us, not kill us. You are lying."* In that moment, I realized that sometimes injustice is not just about what is done, but about the truth that is silenced.

Through it all—the beauty of Barbados, the heartbreak of losing my mother-in-law, the sting of rejection at work, and the devastation of my cousin's death—I learned that life will always bring waves of joy and pain. What matters most is how we stand when those waves crash. Each trial deepened my resilience and shaped the strength I carry forward.

REFLECTIONS

1. Moments of joy are sacred. Life may never be perfect, but we can choose to treasure the perfect moments we are given.

2. Self-control is strength. Calmness in the face of challenges allows us to respond with wisdom instead of reaction.

3. Loss teaches us love. The death of my mother-in-law reminded me to cherish those who treat us with kindness and to hold tightly to the gift of family.

4. Rejection can fuel determination. Sometimes people will doubt us, but their disbelief can become the fire that pushes us to excel.

5. Grief can transform into courage. Losing my cousin reminded me to speak against injustice, even in the face of pain.

6. Resilience is built in storms. Each trial, though painful, deepens our capacity to endure, to rise, and to continue forward with faith.

Chapter 12

When Doors Close, Greater Ones Open

The funeral of my cousin left me broken in ways I could not explain. His absence silenced the laughter, the stories, and the joy he carried wherever he went. I could hardly believe that I would never see him again. His brother, Orlando, was devastated. They had shared an unshakable bond, always looking out for each other. But tragedy came swiftly once more. One afternoon, while downtown Kingston on Ocean Boulevard, Orlando got into a confrontation. In a cruel turn of fate, he was pushed into the sea—unable to swim, he drowned. It was too much grief in such a short span of time. My heart asked questions my mind could not answer. *Why is this happening to our family? Who will be next?*

I turned to God in those moments of despair. I asked Him to sprinkle love into the hearts of mankind, to remind us all to be kinder, gentler, and more compassionate. For I knew that if humanity gave more love, more blessings, and more joy, the world would be a better place. I clung to the truth that God has a solution for every problem, a shadow for every sorrow, and a plan for every tomorrow. That day, I prayed to Him, not from a place of distance but as my closest friend. I thanked Him for His love, even as I asked for strength and renewal of heart.

In my conversation with God, I came to understand something profound: that our desires must align with His desires. If the answer to my prayer does not glorify Him, it is not denial—it is protection. His promises are sure. He satisfies us with good things, renews our youth, and never leaves us without hope.

A DOORWAY TO CANADA AND LESSONS IN RESILIENCE

One day, I tried calling Donald's cousin, Conroy, but he didn't answer, so I left him a message. Three days later, he returned my call. During our conversation, I told him about the passing of my cousin, and he offered his condolences. Then, almost unexpectedly, he asked if I would consider coming to Canada to work with him, since he owned a restaurant. Donald had mentioned to him at his aunt's funeral that I was a chef, and Conroy thought it would be a good opportunity for me. We had spoken briefly about food before, and I even promised to share some recipes with him. Now, here he was, extending a hand of opportunity.

Conroy told me that his wife would write me an invitation letter so I could take it to the embassy. I gathered all the documents—bank statements, police record, and everything else they required. Within two days, the invitation arrived, and I submitted my application. I waited six long weeks for a reply, only to be turned down. The embassy stated that I had no "ties" to my country. Disappointed, I called Conroy to tell him the news. He encouraged me not to give up, promising that we would try again in six months. When his mother later sent another invitation, I applied again, but was denied a second time.

It was at that moment that I realized if I truly wanted to pursue this dream, I would need to create undeniable ties to my homeland. A friend in Rock Hall told me about a piece of land for sale, and I decided to buy it. The property belonged to someone in England, and after speaking with the owner, I went to the National Housing Trust (NHT) to begin the process. With their support, I secured 1.5 million dollars to purchase the land. Owning property gave me a deeper sense of responsibility and stability. I knew this would strengthen my case at the embassy.

When I applied again, I was nervous. Having faced rejection twice before, walking into the embassy to collect my passport on my third try felt heavy. I asked the gentleman at the counter to open the envelope for me, but he refused, insisting that I had to do it myself. When he finally tore it open, he joked that I had been denied again, but then smiled and said, "Congratulations, you got a five-year entry." Tears of joy ran down my face. I couldn't contain myself. That day, I didn't go to work. Instead, I went home, cooked a lovely meal, celebrated with Donald, and later called Conroy with the good news. After three attempts, my dream had become a reality. I loved my job at JUTC, but I knew I was now in a new season.

A JOURNEY OF FAITH: FINDING STRENGTH IN FOREIGN PLACES

In 2014, I bought my ticket and took a leap of faith that would change the course of my life. I boarded a flight to Canada—a breathtakingly beautiful country, filled with both promise and the unknown. When I arrived, Conroy was waiting at the airport with a warm smile and open arms. He drove me to Brampton, where he lived with his family, and from the moment I entered their home, they welcomed me as one of their own.

His wife was especially kind. The very next day, she took me to the mall, where we spent the afternoon together. She even bought me some T-shirts to wear to work at the restaurant. I felt hopeful and grateful—ready to begin this new chapter.

The following morning, she accompanied me to the restaurant, where Conroy worked. Everyone seemed pleasantly surprised to see me. I was introduced to Conroy's mother, whom everyone affectionately called "Grandma," and to the rest of the restaurant team. That day, I stayed behind to observe the flow of operations and get a feel for the environment. By Monday, I began working full-time. It didn't take long for me to notice that the restaurant needed improvement. The food lacked flavor and presentation, yet people still lined up to buy it. I soon realized why—many Canadians simply didn't cook at home. I decided to make small changes each day, using the culinary skills and passion I had brought with me. Slowly but surely, things began to change.

When I prepared the meals, I did so with love, care, and precision. Customers began to notice the difference. The taste was richer, the presentation more vibrant, and soon the restaurant became one of the most talked-about spots in Mississauga. People traveled from far and wide just to taste our red peas soup, oxtail, curry goat, and brown stew fish. There was an elderly gentleman who came every Saturday just for the soup. One day, after taking a spoonful, he looked up at me and said, "This is the best it's ever been. You must be the new chef." When I smiled and nodded, he said, "Keep up the good work—continue to give your best." Before leaving, he handed me his phone number and told me to call him so we could talk more.

The Struggle is Real

By this time, I had been in Canada for a few months and was preparing to go back home. I was working hard and doing my best. Yet inside, I was weary—physically, emotionally, and spiritually. I was working fifteen-hour days for just $400 a week. At first, I thought that was a fair wage, but when I spoke with some other family members, they helped me realize that, given the number of hours I was putting in, it was deeply unfair.

Life had become a cycle of endless work. I went from home to the restaurant and back again, with no time to rest or even explore the beauty of the country I had dreamed of seeing. Grandma and I shared the same living space, and every night, she would sit in front of the television for one and a half to two hours before heading to the washroom, knowing I had to wake up at 6:00 a.m. to prepare breakfast for the restaurant. Many nights, I went to bed at 2:00 a.m. and woke just a few hours later, exhausted but determined to press on. I often felt invisible—like no one truly cared about how drained I was. It seemed as though the only thing that mattered was keeping the business running.

But through it all, God was with me. Even in my weariness, I felt His quiet strength guiding me through each day. He was teaching me endurance, patience, and self-worth. Though I felt trapped between duty and exhaustion, I learned that sometimes God uses difficult seasons to build resilience within us.

When I finally told Conroy that I wanted to go home, it wasn't out of anger—I was very grateful for the opportunity. I knew in my heart that my purpose extended beyond that kitchen and beyond that season.

Looking back, I realize that it was not failure that sent me home—it was faith. Sometimes, God will place you in uncomfortable spaces not to punish you, but to prepare you. That experience taught me courage, discernment, and the importance of knowing when to walk away. It taught me that no matter where you go, your worth travels with you.

REFLECTIONS

1. **Grief is a Teacher** – Losing loved ones reshapes us. It teaches us that life is fragile and time is precious. In grief, God whispers that He is our ultimate comforter.

2. **Delay is Not Denial** – Two visa refusals could have broken me, but they were simply redirections. When God finally opened the door, it was with firmer roots and greater purpose.

3. **Faith Requires Action** – I did not just pray; I purchased land, secured my documents, and positioned myself for opportunity. Faith works when we work alongside it.

4. **Value Yourself** – Never allow others to determine your worth. Know your value and stand by it.

5. **God Sends Helpers** – Sometimes family fails, but strangers step in as divine helpers. Trust that God will place the right people in your path.

6. **New Beginnings Require Courage** – Moving to Canada was not easy, but it was the soil where my faith, resilience, and vision were tested and strengthened.

Chapter 13

Returning, Rebuilding, and Rising Stronger

FINDING YOUR INNER STRENGTH

One day, during a heartfelt conversation with my father, he mentioned that I had relatives living in Canada. My heart lifted with curiosity and hope. A few days later, he arranged for me to meet them, and that afternoon, I found myself face-to-face with three of my family members. Their excitement upon seeing me was contagious—we exchanged numbers and warm embraces. Though our meeting was brief, as I had to return to work, it left a lasting impression on my heart.

Later, I called Uncle Tyrone to share what I was experiencing—the long hours, the mistreatment at the restaurant, and the growing sense that it was time for me to return home. He listened patiently and gently advised me, but when I told him I had made up my mind, he completely respected my decision. That was something I always admired about him—his humility, understanding, and quiet wisdom. It felt good to finally connect with that side of my father's family; it gave me a sense of belonging I hadn't realized I needed.

That same night, I called Donald and told him everything that had been happening. He immediately said, "Come home." His voice gave me strength, and the next morning I decided—I was going back. When I told my boss at the restaurant, he was upset, though I couldn't understand why. After all, they were the ones who had treated me unfairly. I continued to work until my departure day, which fell on a Friday. My flight was at noon, but I worked fourteen hours that night and stayed up packing the rest of the time. Early the next morning, I was asked to leave the house because everyone was heading out early. I stood outside in the freezing cold, luggage beside me, waiting for my ride. Before leaving, I turned to Grandma and expressed my gratitude for her hospitality and kindness during my stay. Tears welled up in her eyes as I said goodbye.

I waited in the cold for two long hours before my ride arrived. Together, we went to the restaurant to collect the two weeks' pay that was owed to me. To my disbelief, the boss claimed he had no money and told me to leave before he called the police. I was stunned. How could he threaten me like that after all the hours I had worked? I knew his actions were driven by malice—he was aware that my paperwork wasn't complete, and he used that as leverage.

My friend, sensing my frustration, whispered, "Lavern, come. It's getting late—you'll miss your flight."

I took a deep breath, smiled through the pain, and said to the boss, "Thank you for your hospitality. May God bless you richly." Those words weren't sarcastic—they came from a place of release. I chose peace over bitterness.

I handed my friend 60 Canadian dollars for gas, and he was grateful—he, too, was struggling at the time. I hugged him tightly and began to cry. He whispered, "Don't worry. Everything will be fine. Leave it all in God's hands."

When I boarded that flight and saw Donald waiting at the airport in Jamaica, a wave of relief washed over me; every burden I had carried seemed to lift. Seeing his face reminded me that no matter where life takes you, love and support can heal the deepest wounds. Everyone was happy to see me, especially Donald's father.

THE POWER OF STARTING AGAIN

Back in Jamaica, life was quieter but uncertain. I had no job since I had resigned to pursue the opportunity in Canada. I was disappointed, even ashamed, but I reminded myself that life goes on. Despite everything, I was home—and there was a peace in that. Canada had left me weary and stressed, but Jamaica gave me rest, sunlight, and familiarity.

My family in Canada stayed in touch, checking in on me often. Mr. John, a kind-hearted friend, would even send me money when I told him things were slow. He asked if I planned to return to Canada and whether I had relatives there who could host me. I told him about reconnecting with my father's side of the family, and he encouraged me to reach out.

When I spoke with Uncle Tyrone, I explained my desire to come back to Canada but admitted that I had nowhere to stay. He told me he only had one bedroom, but would ask Aunt Lurline on my behalf. She lived alone in a three-bedroom home and agreed to host me. Uncle Tyrone cautioned, "She's not the easiest person to live with, but give it a try." I decided to take the chance. I immediately called Mr. John and told him the family said yes.

A few weeks later, I was back on a plane—hopeful that this time would be different. Mr. John picked me up from the airport and drove me to Aunt Lurline's home in Brampton. When we arrived, we went inside together and I introduced him to my aunt. Her facial expression changed quickly; it was as if she disapproved of him at first glance. *Perhaps it was the color of his skin*, I thought to myself. Stereotyping, I realized, is such a shallow thing—you can't judge a book by its cover. You have to open it first to understand what is inside.

After Mr. John left, Aunt Lurline asked where I knew him from and said she "didn't like his spirit." I quietly changed the subject. She began telling me about other family members and showed me to my room. The next morning, she made breakfast, and soon after, Uncle Tyrone came by. The three of us talked for hours—it felt good to share laughter again.

Uncle Tyrone helped me find a job at a restaurant called Jamaica House. He took me there himself and introduced me to the owner. The first question asked was, "Young lady, can you cook?" I smiled and replied, "Give me a chance." He handed me a bowl of batter and asked me to fry some fritters. I forgot to add baking powder, so they turned out a bit hard—but still edible. He laughed and said, "You'll do." I was hired. From that day forward, I worked hard to prove myself. I learned to prepare breakfast, clean the kitchen, and multitask efficiently. My coworker showed me the ropes, and though it was challenging, I was grateful.

Every morning, I took three buses from Brampton to Finch, leaving home early to ensure I arrived by 8:00 a.m. One snowy morning, I was ten minutes late and was scolded for it. From that day on, I left home at 5:00 a.m., determined never to be late again. I needed that job—and I respected it. Even after long days of work and long commutes, I always took time to sit and talk with Aunt Pauline when I got home. It became our little routine. I wanted her to know I appreciated her generosity, and deep down, I sensed she valued the company.

One evening, everything changed. I came home to find her upset. It was snowing outside, and she said, "You sicken my stomach. The blood of Jesus is against you. You can't stay here any longer." I was shocked. I asked what I had done wrong, but she gave no answer—just repeated, "You have to go." I reminded her that I was paying her 300 Canadian dollars in rent, but she refused to listen. Confused and hurt, I called Uncle Tyrone, who told me calmly, "Go to your room and ignore her." The next day, I went to work feeling drained and depressed. That evening, Uncle Tyrone came to speak with her. She told him I had "no manners," which was not true. Other family members also called and tried to reason with her, insisting that I be allowed to stay until I found another place. But Aunt Lurline refused. That weekend, Uncle Tyrone came for me and took me to stay with Aunt Winsome in Pickering.

A few days later, while riding the bus, I met a friend who was a regular customer at the restaurant. When I told him my situation, he said he knew of a room for rent—a small one-bedroom with a shared kitchen and bathroom for 400 Canadian dollars. I said yes immediately.

I moved in with nothing but my clothes—no bed, no furniture, no comfort—but I had peace. Uncle Tyrone helped me buy a bed, and slowly, things began to fall into place. Life wasn't easy, but it was mine. For the first time, I had space to think, breathe, and manage my own life. I worked hard, built consistency, and found a rhythm that gave me strength. Through it all, Uncle Tyrone remained my anchor. He checked in often, took me to new places, and reminded me, "Be careful and keep your faith strong." His support became a symbol of divine provision—a reminder that even when some doors close, God always sends the right people to open new ones.

REFLECTIONS

1. **Grace in Adversity** – True strength is not measured by revenge but by the ability to respond with dignity when treated unjustly.

2. **Family as Anchor** – Even imperfect family connections can provide grounding, wisdom, and encouragement when life feels overwhelming.

3. **Resilience Through Struggle** – Hardship teaches us resourcefulness. Every early morning bus ride, every rejection, and every setback was shaping discipline and character.

4. **Finding Freedom in Independence** – Sometimes being alone is the doorway to clarity and growth. Standing on your own allows you to discover your true capacity.

5. **Faith as the Foundation** – When human support falters, God remains constant. Trusting His timing and plan transforms obstacles into stepping stones.

Chapter 14

New Paths, New Promises

PURSUING THE PATH OF CARE

There are moments in life when a simple opportunity becomes the doorway to destiny. For me, that moment came when I heard about a school offering training for Personal Support Workers (PSW). I had always loved caring for others, especially the elderly, so the thought of becoming a PSW stirred something deep within me.

My uncle, ever supportive, took me to the school to register. I told my friend, Ms. Quen, about it, and she decided to join me. We began the course together, and though the journey was demanding, it was filled with purpose. I was working two jobs while attending classes—exhausting, yes, but I had set my mind on success. When you are determined to reach your goals, no obstacle can hold you back. Every hardship becomes another step toward becoming who you are meant to be.

As we neared the end of our training, we began our practical placements and volunteer hours—120 hours of service and six weeks of hands-on experience at Western Garden and Western Terrace Nursing Homes. Those were long days, but fulfilling ones.

I worked mornings and attended classes in the evenings, often running on little sleep but plenty of passion. My preceptor noticed my dedication and told me, *"You are an excellent PSW—you have a gift for this."* Her words filled me with pride and gratitude. I knew then that I was walking in purpose, not just completing a course.

There were many nights when I would ride the bus or train home late, weary from work and study. But Ms. Quen was always there—calling to keep me company until she was sure I was home safely. She became my anchor in those difficult days, a true friend who reminded me that I was not alone. I often told her she was my hero. She was the first real friend I had when I came to Canada, and her kindness and consistency became a lifeline. From her, I learned that strength is not about being unshakable—it's about standing tall, even when you're tired and continuing to move forward with humility and faith. She taught me that perseverance always pays off, that if you remain patient and true to yourself, your moment of success will come. Life may not always be easy, but every season of struggle prepares you for a season of strength.

A COMPLETE CHANGE IN LIFE TRAJECTORY

As time passed, reality began to settle in: I was now in Canada as a landed immigrant, and my life had truly taken root here. I had no intention of returning home, especially since I had resigned from my job in Jamaica before coming. I knew it was time to make a firm decision about my future. During this period, I met someone who changed the course of my life. After much prayer and conversation, we decided to get married. When I told my uncle, he asked if I was sure. I told him that I had found peace in the decision—we both knew what we wanted and had already set the date. Our wedding was planned for May 23rd, 2016, at my cousin's church on Weston

Road. One of the church members helped with the decorations, and her attention to detail made everything beautiful. My friend, Harry, along with his co-worker, took charge of preparing the food, and they did an incredible job.

The menu was a reflection of love and culture—oxtail, curry goat, fried and jerk chicken, brown stew fish, rice and peas, potato salad, garden salad, and even goat head soup. It was a feast of celebration and togetherness. That morning, my dear friend, Ms. Junie, came to help me get ready, doing my makeup and helping me into my dress. When the car arrived to take me to the church, my heart raced with both nerves and joy.

The church looked breathtaking—soft colors, glowing faces, and a presence of peace that only God could have arranged. As I walked down the aisle, I caught sight of my husband-to-be smiling at me, his face radiant with happiness. When the ceremony concluded, I realized that every trial, every cold night, every tear I had shed in the journey to this point had prepared me for this day. I was now a married woman—fulfilled, thankful, and standing in the grace of new beginnings. It was, without question, one of the happiest days of my life.

REFLECTIONS

1. Purpose is found in service. When you pour into others, you discover who you truly are.

2. Determination transforms dreams into reality. Hard work, no matter how exhausting, always pays off.

3. True friendship is rare but priceless. When someone chooses to walk beside you through hardship, treasure them deeply.

4. Every challenge strengthens your faith. Sleepless nights and silent tears are the soil where resilience grows.

5. Love flourishes where faith leads. When you follow God's peace, the path ahead unfolds with divine timing.

6. Gratitude elevates every season. Even in struggle, thankfulness shifts your focus from what's missing to what's possible.

7. Your story is your strength. Every trial is a chapter of transformation—embrace it, for it's shaping your testimony.

Chapter 15

Trials That Shape Resilience

THE GRIEF OF LOSING A LOVED ONE

Life seemed to be testing every fiber of my endurance. I was still working at the restaurant when I got a new opportunity at a nursing home on King Street called *The Brick House*. The interview was brief—the owner took one look at me and said, "You're hired." I began working there four nights a week, Monday to Thursday, from 7:00 p.m. to 7:00 a.m., while still keeping my restaurant job. Two jobs, endless hours, but I had no choice. I needed to get my documentation in order and secure my life in this new land.

One afternoon, while cleaning chicken at the restaurant, I received a call from Jamaica. The words on the other end shattered me—my grandmother had passed away. My body went numb. I dropped everything and stepped outside, trying to catch my breath as grief came crashing down like a wave I couldn't escape. That day, I wasn't myself. A friend of the boss came into the kitchen, teasing and provoking me, even after I told him I wasn't in the mood. His words pierced my fragile state until anger boiled over. I grabbed him by the shirt, still holding the knife I'd been using. Just then, my boss, Mr. Michael, shouted, "No, Lavern! Don't do that! Do you want to go to prison?" His words jolted me back to my senses. I dropped the knife, realizing that I couldn't throw my future away for a man who didn't deserve my energy.

The next day, the boss called me into his office, siding with his friend. I explained what had happened, but his tone made it clear that he had already chosen his side. That weekend, I collected my pay and walked out for the last time. My world fell quiet. My grandmother—my rock, my guide, the woman who raised me—was gone. There was no one to mourn with me in the mornings, no one to comfort me at night. I cried myself to sleep many nights, trying to hide my pain behind strength. Every organ in my body felt heavy, as if grief had settled into my bones. She had always told me to keep working on my papers, to stay strong and focused. Three months before she passed, she'd encouraged me not to give up. Now she was gone, and I couldn't even go home for the funeral. That was the hardest part—knowing that the woman who shaped my life took her last breath without my goodbye. My siblings called daily to check in, and my husband tried his best to comfort me.

On the night of the *nine-night*, the roads in my hometown were blocked—people came from everywhere to pay their respects. She was deeply loved. My grandmother had told me long ago that when she passed, she wanted me to sing. Unable to attend, I watched her funeral through a video call. I had written a speech and I read it over the phone through video. It went like this:

"Pastors, officials, ministers, family members, ladies and gentlemen, boys and girls—good afternoon. My name is Lavern Carr, Mrs. Roy's granddaughter. If I were to use words to describe my Grandma, it would be 'wonderful and gracious Grandma.'

The Struggle is Real

My grandma was always there to lend a helping hand, offer a shoulder to cry on, comfort you in every way, and help you conquer all your fears.

Despite all the wrongs I have done and all the wrongs you will do, my Grandma would always be there, unconditionally loving you.

Mama, my Grandma, was always busy, always doing something. As early as morning, she would be fixing something outside or doing house chores. Mama was a very energetic woman—loving, caring, sharing—and most of all, a compassionate person.

Words can't explain how I feel about my grandma. I wish I were there to show you all. She was truly amazing—a grandma, a mother, a friend, a father, a wife—you name it.

Mama, my great Mama—she's the one who taught me everything I know, from birth to adulthood. She taught me well. Without Mama, we would be lost; our tears would not be dried, and we would not be encouraged to spread our wings and fly.

Grandma, I know that you are in a better place, and I am grateful for the impact you had on my life. I thank you for all the guidance you gave me throughout the years. I thank you, Grandma, for believing in me and for having patience with me. Most of all, I thank you for playing such a big role in my life.

Grandma, I cherish every moment that we spent together, and I'm thankful I have such a wonderful angel looking over me and the rest of the family.

To my grandma, I say thank you. My heart will always be with you every day, and I know you're here with me.

May your soul rest in peace, Grandma."

Though I read these words through the screens, everyone cried. Though I couldn't be there, my heart was home.

WHEN NEW OPPORTUNITIES ARISE

Not long after, a woman named Ms. LV offered me a chef position at a restaurant close to where I lived at the time. I started on a Monday, hopeful. But business was slow, and within a week, she reduced my shifts to four days. Eventually, she sold the restaurant, and I moved on.

Soon after, a friend told me about a new restaurant on Weston Road and Lawrence. I visited, met the owner, Leon, and his colleague Christine. They hired me for their grand opening, and it went beautifully. Customers loved the food, and I began full-time work the following Monday. For three months, everything seemed stable—until family drama surfaced. The restaurant had been opened for Leon's children, but they showed no interest at first. When they eventually came around, tension grew. A friend of mine called one day, tired of her own workplace, and I encouraged her to join me. Leon agreed to hire her, and for a time, we were a team again. We lived far apart—me in Scarborough, her in Jane and Steeles—but I picked her up every morning so we could work together. Then business slowed, and Leon cut her shifts to three days. It didn't make sense for one of us to carry the load alone, so she left, and I followed soon after. I didn't know where I was going, but I knew I couldn't stay.

One afternoon, while waiting outside with my coffee, my phone rang. It was Leon's daughter. She said, "Please come back. The food doesn't taste the same, and the customers are complaining." I hesitated but agreed to return. Within weeks, business revived, and customers told me how much they missed my cooking. Soon, Leon said he wanted to sell the restaurant and asked if I would buy it. I didn't have the funds, but my pastor's cousin was interested. He purchased it, and I stayed on to manage it with my friend.

LESSONS OF COMPASSION AND COURAGE

Two months later, the pastor's wife's niece joined the team. She worked hard but was underpaid and overworked. I spoke up, telling him it wasn't right to treat people like that. One day, he accused me of disrespecting the cashier. I left in frustration, and my friend refused to return without me. A few days later, the pastor called, apologizing and asking me to come back. My heart softened, as it often does, and I returned with Ms. Quen. It amazed me how often people who mistreated me ended up needing me again. Life has a way of turning the tables. I realized that what is yours will always return to you—no one can take it away.

But soon, business slowed again. The pastor began cutting hours, including mine and Ms. Quen's. His cousin Kevin arrived from overseas with his wife and two kids to help run the restaurant, but money troubles continued. Eventually, disagreements erupted, and my friend left. When I learned that the pastor planned to sell the restaurant, I asked him what would happen to his family living in the basement. His response was cold—he claimed he had no choice. My heart broke for them, especially their little girl, whom I had grown close to. When they had nowhere else to go, I opened my one-bedroom home to them. I slept on the sofa so they could have the bedroom. For four months, I did everything I could to keep them safe. That is what my grandmother taught me—to do for others what I would hope someone might do for me.

One evening, I learned that the little girl was being bitten at night. I searched the room and discovered bed bugs. I was horrified. I reported it, but even after two treatments, the problem persisted. I had to throw out nearly all my furniture. For seven months, I slept on the floor in an empty apartment, paying 1,370 Canadian dollars in rent for a place that no longer felt like home.

When my cousin, Portia, arrived from Jamaica and saw my living conditions, she was heartbroken. I told her, "This is one thing I never want anyone—friend or enemy—to experience." It was one of the hardest seasons of my life.

REFLECTIONS

1. Grief tests the soul, but it also purifies it. Through tears, we learn resilience.

2. Every ending carries a seed of rebirth. Walking away often makes space for better beginnings.

3. People will hurt you, and some will return humbled. Choose grace, not bitterness—it's your strength, not your weakness.

4. True compassion costs something. But the heart that gives freely never runs empty.

5. Adversity is the teacher of wisdom. Even in hardship, you are being shaped into the person your destiny requires you to be.

Chapter 16

The Courage to Keep Moving Forward

RISING THROUGH THE SEASONS

I've always been one to socialize easily and adapt to different environments. A friend of mine called and asked if I was working, and when I told him I was looking for a job, he directed me to an interview. I went with two others—Money and Lisa—and after submitting my police check and driver's license, I was hired as a shuttle driver.

It was exhilarating. I drove everything from Maserati and Ferrari to Lexus, BMW, Jeep, and Mercedes-Benz—vehicles most people only dream of sitting in. For me, it was not just a job; it was a chance to experience a different world, even if for a moment.

When winter came, the glamour faded and the grind took over. The workload shifted from driving to clearing snow, moving vehicles, cleaning the shop, and detailing cars in freezing temperatures. My hands would grow numb from the cold, but I pressed on. It wasn't about pride—it was about purpose.

Even as a woman in a male-dominated workspace, I stood firm, doing everything asked of me. Yet, over time, the tone of the workplace changed. The respect I once felt began to fade. The words grew harsh, and I realized it was time to move on. I handed my resignation to Lisa and made one of the boldest decisions of my life—to go back to school.

A NEW CHAPTER OF LEARNING

On February 4, 2019, I began a new journey at Emery Adult Learning Centre in North York, Ontario. When I arrived, I discovered that the classes were held during the day, not evenings as I had expected. I stood there wondering, *How will I balance this with work?*

But my best friend encouraged me. She said, "This is your dream. Go for it. God will work it out." Those words stayed with me. I decided to trust the process and step forward in faith. It wasn't easy. I faced financial struggles, exhaustion, and endless sleepless nights. I worked twelve-hour night shifts, then went straight to school for seven more hours in the morning. But I never missed a class. I valued every moment, every lesson, every opportunity to learn.

My English teacher was exceptional—clear, patient, and deeply inspiring. One of our assigned novels was about Ishmael Beah, a young boy forced to become a child soldier at just thirteen years old. His story of pain, trauma, and redemption moved me deeply. As I read, I saw reflections of my own resilience—how we both turned our pain into purpose. That novel inspired me to write my own story, to give voice to my struggles and victories, and to show others that healing and greatness can rise from hardship.

Later, we studied another novel, *No New Land*, which told the story of a family that migrated to Canada seeking a better life, only to face discrimination, racism, and disappointment. Reading it felt like reading chapters of my own life. I, too, had faced the silent battles of being an immigrant—fighting to belong, to prove my worth, and to stay hopeful in a system that didn't always see me. Through these stories, I learned that pain has a purpose and knowledge is one of the greatest forms of liberation.

FAITH, FRIENDSHIP, AND FINDING STRENGTH

Life as an immigrant is a balancing act—between hope and heartbreak, between progress and pain. I continued to work hard and eventually joined an agency called Tranquil Care, where I met Gobebe, a humble and selfless man from Nigeria. He helped me update my résumé, supported my studies, and checked in often to make sure I was okay. His kindness reminded me that genuine people still exist in this world.

Through determination, I bought myself a 2018 RAV4, fulfilling one of my long-time dreams. My next goal was to own a home. I worked seven nights a week and attended school five days a week. It was difficult, but I kept my eyes fixed on the vision.

One evening, I received a call from the agency to work a one-on-one shift with a patient named Marie at Providence Healthcare. Meeting her was like meeting an angel. Marie reminded me of my grandmother—gentle, wise, and full of grace. She told me something I'll never forget: *"When the storms come your way, remember—you know the Master of the wind. When sickness finds you, remember—you know the Great Physician. When your heart is broken, say to yourself—I know the Potter."*

Marie's words anchored me. She reminded me that true wealth isn't in titles, degrees, or money, but in kindness, integrity, and humility. Now, when I smile, it's not because life is perfect—it's because I've learned to be grateful for what I have. I've fought countless battles, cried a thousand tears, and still found reasons to rise again. I've been broken, betrayed, abandoned, and rejected, yet I remain unshaken in faith and steadfast in purpose.

REFLECTIONS

1. Your struggles are not setbacks—they are setups for strength. Every season of difficulty builds resilience and shapes your destiny.

2. Hardship refines humility. The greatest victories are born from the deepest valleys.

3. Faith is your anchor. When you trust that God stands for you, no force can stand against you.

4. Be grateful for genuine souls. People like Marie and Gabebe are reminders that light still lives among us.

5. Never stop believing in your dreams. The path may be long and cold, but better days are always ahead.

Chapter 17

The Legacy of a Life Well Lived

LESSONS THAT SHAPE THE SOUL

This world is full of good people; if you cannot find one, then be one. Every lesson changes us, shaping who we are and how we see others. It is easy to judge the mistakes of others, yet far more difficult to recognize our own. No one has the right to judge you because no one truly knows the battles you have fought. They may have heard your story, but they have never felt your pain. Success embraces you in private, while failure often shames you in public—that is the nature of life. The difference between school and life is this: in school, you are taught a lesson and then given a test; in life, you are tested first, and through that test, you learn the lesson.

Keep your distance from people who refuse to admit when they are wrong and who try to make you feel like you are the problem. Never beg for attention or force someone to remember you—simply be still and let your absence teach them the value of your presence. If you fail, never give up. Remember that F.A.I.L. means *First Attempt In Learning*. When you reach what feels like the end, know that E.N.D. means *Effort Never Dies*. If someone says "no," take it as Next Opportunity. Every closed door hides a new beginning waiting for your persistence to open it.

Do not compare your journey to others. There is no comparison between the sun and the moon—they both shine at their appointed time. To be successful, you do not need a beautiful face or everyone's approval; what you need is a wise mind, a kind heart, and the courage to act. Train your thoughts to see the good in every situation. The quality of your thinking determines the quality of your life. Always remember two important things: take care of your thoughts when you are alone, and take care of your words when you are with others.

The best revenge is no revenge—move on and be happy. The greatest test in life is having the patience to wait for the right moment. A clear rejection is always better than a false promise. Never stop learning, for life never stops teaching. Life becomes easier when you learn to accept an apology you never received. Never laugh at someone else's hardship, because one day you may find yourself in a similar place.

Always walk with the Lord when your heart needs company. Take His hand when you feel alone. Turn to Him when you need someone to lean on, for He will never leave you. God will carry you through every storm, strengthen you in every battle, and bring peace to your heart. Believe in yourself and in the power of the One who lives within you.

REFLECTIONS

1. **Empathy Over Judgment** – Understand that everyone carries unseen burdens; choose compassion over criticism.

2. **Every Failure is a Lesson** – Life's tests reveal what we need to learn for the next season.

3. **Perspective Shapes Reality** – How you see challenges determines how you overcome them.

4. **Guard Your Words and Thoughts** – Discipline in speech and thought preserves character and peace.

5. **Faith is the Ultimate Anchor** – Trusting God provides strength, direction, and joy, even in storms.

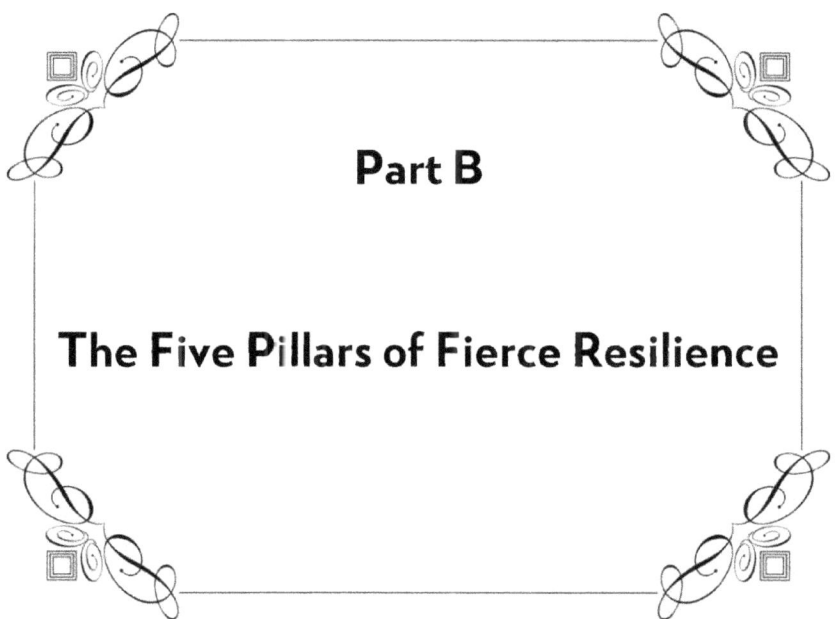

Part B

The Five Pillars of Fierce Resilience

Chapter 18

A Framework for Unshakeable Strength and Unstoppable Faith

RESILIENCE – THE POWER TO RISE AGAIN

If you've made it this far in this book, it means you've walked through something, maybe even crawled through it. You've felt pressure, pain, and the weight of moments that almost broke you. You've had seasons that stretched you so thin, you wondered how you'd ever come back from it. But here you are, still standing, still breathing, still showing up. That right there is resilience.

Resilience isn't about never falling. It's about *what you do when you hit the ground.* It's about that quiet strength that rises when everything else falls apart. It's not the loud roar of victory—it's the whisper that says, *"I'm not done yet."*

We often think resilience means we have to be tough all the time—like we can't cry, feel, or fall apart. But that's not true resilience. Real resilience isn't about pretending you're fine; it's about allowing yourself to feel the pain, learn from it, and still move forward. It's the balance between breaking and rebuilding, and finding beauty in both.

Resilience is the comeback story written in the middle of chaos. It's not about bouncing back to who you used to be; it's about *becoming someone new* because of what you've been through. You're not meant to go back; you're meant to grow forward.

WHEN LIFE KNOCKS YOU DOWN

There are moments when life will test every part of you: your faith, patience, confidence, and hope. It's in those moments you find out what you're really made of. Sometimes it's not until everything shakes that we realize how strong our foundation truly is.

You've probably had times when you said, *"I can't take one more thing,"* and then something else happened. Yet, somehow, you still made it through. That's not luck—that's your God-given resilience. It's the part of you that refuses to give up, even when giving up feels easier.

Every challenge you've faced has been shaping something inside you. The struggle was never to destroy you; it was to *develop you*. It taught you how to adapt, how to recover, and how to rebuild with wisdom. Every time you got back up, you became stronger, not just in your mind, but in your spirit.

WHAT RESILIENCE REALLY LOOKS LIKE

Resilience looks like wiping your tears, fixing your crown, and trying again. It looks like getting up the next morning, even though your heart is still heavy. It looks like saying, *"I don't know how this will work out, but I believe somehow it will."* It's not about always being okay—it's about trusting that even in the not-okay moments, something good is still being formed.

Resilience is built in the hard places—the waiting, the heartbreak, the disappointments. It grows in silence and shows itself in strength. Every setback, every loss, every delay—all of it trained you to become who you are now. It's the very thing that gave you wisdom, compassion, and depth. You might not have chosen what happened to you, but you can choose how you rise from it.

THE TRANSFORMATION IN THE STRUGGLE

There's a point in every journey where you realize the struggle wasn't meant to stop you—it was meant to *shape you.* You begin to see that every obstacle carried a lesson. You stop asking "Why me?" and start asking "What is this teaching me?"

The truth is, the struggle is real, but so is your strength.

Resilience teaches you that pain can have purpose, and endings can lead to new beginnings. It helps you see that every time something fell apart, it made room for something better to be built.

When you understand resilience, you stop being afraid of falling, because you know you can rise again. You stop being afraid of failure because you've learned that failure can be the beginning of something greater.

YOU ARE LIVING PROOF

The fact that you're still here means you've already proven your resilience. You've overcome things that others may never know about. You've survived nights of tears, days of doubt, and seasons that tested your soul. But you made it, not by chance, but by courage. And that's what resilience is: courage in motion.

It's your decision to keep walking, even when the path isn't clear. It's your faith that, even after loss, love will rise again. It's your belief that no matter how hard the chapter, the story isn't over yet.

You are living proof that resilience works. You've already been practicing it: now it's time to strengthen it intentionally.

INTRODUCING THE FIVE PILLARS OF FIERCE RESILIENCE

In the next section, I'll walk you through what I call **The Five Pillars of Fierce Resilience**; the foundation that helps you stand tall when life tries to knock you down.

These pillars aren't theories; they're truths I've lived. They're lessons built from the pain, the pressure, and the perseverance it took to rise again. Each one will help you rebuild your confidence, regain your clarity, and reignite your purpose.

If you've ever wondered how to move from surviving to thriving—from barely holding on to walking in strength—these five pillars are your roadmap. Because resilience isn't just about getting through, it's about *growing through*. Now it's time to discover how.

The Five Pillars of Fierce Resilience

A FRAMEWORK FOR UNSHAKEABLE STRENGTH
AND UNSTOPPABLE FAITH

Pillar 1

Faith Beyond Feelings – Anchoring Your Soul in the Storm

There comes a point in everyone's life where what you *believe* will be tested by what you *feel*.

When life feels unpredictable—when the plan falls apart, when the prayer feels unanswered, when you're tired of pretending you're okay—that's where *faith beyond feelings* begins.

Faith beyond feelings doesn't mean ignoring what's real. It means acknowledging your emotions without allowing them to lead your decisions. It's saying, *"I feel uncertain, but I still choose to believe that something good can come from this."*

Let's be honest—feelings are powerful, but they're also temporary. They rise and fall like waves, but faith is the anchor that keeps you from drifting when everything else starts to move. When you learn to lead with faith instead of feelings, you stop being controlled by the chaos around you. You start to find peace, even when the storm hasn't passed.

WHEN FAITH FEELS HARD

There will be days when your faith feels thin—when you've prayed, planned, and pushed and nothing seems to change. Maybe you've said to yourself, *"I'm doing everything right, so why is everything going wrong?"*

I've been there too.

I've stared at closed doors and wondered if I missed my chance. I've looked at my bank account and felt fear rise in my throat. I've questioned my path, worth, and purpose. But it was in those moments that I discovered what faith really is. Faith isn't proven when everything's easy—it's forged when everything feels impossible.

Faith beyond feelings says, *"I may not see it, but I still believe it."* It's that quiet conviction that whispers, *"There's more to this moment than what I feel right now."*

FAITH IS A MUSCLE, NOT A MOOD

Faith isn't something you either have or don't have—it's something you *build*.

Every disappointment, every delay, every detour is a workout for your belief system. It's training your trust to stretch beyond what's comfortable. Think of it this way: every time you choose to keep going instead of giving up, your faith grows stronger. Every time you decide to hope again after being hurt, your faith builds endurance. You don't have to *feel* strong to *be* strong. You just have to take one small step of trust—again and again—until faith becomes your default response instead of fear.

FAITH AND REALITY CAN COEXIST

Faith doesn't deny the reality of your situation, it simply refuses to be limited by it.

You can admit, *"This hurts,"* and still believe, *"But I'll heal."*

You can acknowledge, *"I don't know how,"* and still trust, *"But I'll find a way."*

Too often, we think faith means pretending everything is fine. But faith doesn't require fake strength, it requires *real surrender*. It's saying, *"I don't have all the answers, but I trust there's a reason for this season."* Faith doesn't erase emotions; it gives emotions direction. It turns panic into prayer, worry into wisdom, and fear into fuel.

HOW TO STRENGTHEN FAITH BEYOND FEELINGS

If you want your faith to be more than a feeling, you must *practice* it like a skill. Here's how you begin:

1. Shift from reaction to reflection.

Instead of reacting to every emotion, take a pause. Ask yourself, *"What truth am I standing on right now?"* Sometimes what feels true in the moment isn't the whole story.

2. Revisit your proof.

Think back to all the times you thought you wouldn't make it, yet, somehow, you did. Those moments are your evidence. They remind you that faith has carried you before, and it can carry you again.

3. Speak what you want to see.

Words shape belief. Each morning, try saying out loud: *"My faith is stronger than my feelings. I am grounded, I am growing, and I am guided."*

You may not *feel* it the first time, but keep saying it. Your words will eventually catch up with your reality.

FAITH IN ACTION

Faith beyond feelings doesn't mean life gets easier—it means *you get steadier.* You begin to respond differently to challenges because you understand that what's happening *to* you might actually be happening *for* you.

You start to recognize that the waiting, the silence, the setbacks—they all have purpose. Faith reframes your pain as part of the process, and little by little, the storms that once shook you start to strengthen you instead.

REFLECTION QUESTIONS

When was the last time you let your feelings dictate your decisions? What did that cost you?

_____
_____
_____
_____
_____

What situation in your life right now is requiring you to trust beyond what you can see?

_____
_____
_____
_____
_____

What truth can you remind yourself of daily to anchor your faith?

_____
_____
_____
_____
_____
_____
_____

CLOSING THOUGHT

Faith beyond feelings is the foundation of fierce resilience. It's what holds you steady when emotions fluctuate and circumstances shift. It's not about denying reality, it's about daring to believe that there's something greater unfolding beyond what you can see.

You don't need to have it all figured out. You just need enough faith to take the next step. Sometimes, the smallest act of belief in the middle of the storm is the very thing that brings you through it.

Pillar 2

Courage in Chaos – Standing Firm When Life Falls Apart

Chaos has a way of showing up uninvited. One moment everything seems to be falling into place, and the next, it's all falling apart. Life rarely gives us notice before it shifts, and sometimes the very ground beneath us starts to move without warning. That's when courage steps in. Courage in chaos isn't loud. It doesn't always look like bold speeches or fearless faces. Sometimes, it's simply the quiet decision to keep showing up when everything in you wants to shut down. It's the whisper that says, *"I don't know how I'll make it through this…but I will."* When life is unpredictable, courage is what steadies your soul. It reminds you that even in the middle of uncertainty, you still have power—the power to choose, to move, to believe, and to become.

COURAGE DOESN'T CANCEL FEAR, IT RISES ABOVE IT

So many people wait for fear to disappear before they act. They tell themselves, *"When I feel ready, I'll take the step."* But here's the truth: you may never feel ready. Courage isn't about waiting for confidence, it's about moving while afraid. Fear and courage often show up on the same battlefield. The difference is which one you listen to.

Fear says, *"You're not enough."*

Courage says, *"Maybe not yet, but I'm growing."*

Fear says, *"What if you fail?"*

Courage whispers, *"What if you fly?"*

Every time you take a step despite your fear, you weaken its hold on your life. Every time you speak when your voice shakes, stand when your knees tremble, or begin again after falling apart, that's courage in action. It's not that the fear is gone. It's that *you chose to move anyway.*

THE LESSON HIDDEN IN CHAOS

Chaos is not always the enemy. Sometimes it's the teacher that shakes up your life to reveal what's unsteady within you. It strips away false confidence and exposes where your strength truly lies. When everything feels like it's falling apart, it might actually be falling into place, just not in the way you expected. Think of the moments in your life when things didn't go according to plan—the relationship that ended, the job that didn't last, the door that slammed shut. At first, it felt like chaos. But looking back, can you see how that disruption redirected you to something better? That's the quiet wisdom of courage: it looks chaos in the eye and says, *"I trust that something good is being built out of this mess."*

THE COURAGE TO LET GO

One of the hardest forms of courage is learning when to let go—of control, of outcomes, of what you thought life was supposed to look like. We often cling to what's familiar, even when it's painful, because uncertainty scares us more than struggle. But growth doesn't come from gripping tighter; it comes from releasing what no longer fits your future. Courage means accepting that not everything broken needs to be fixed by you. Sometimes peace arrives when you finally stop fighting what's trying to change you. Letting go doesn't mean giving up. It means making room for what's next.

HOW TO BUILD COURAGE IN CHAOS

Here are some ways to strengthen your inner steadiness when everything feels uncertain:

1. **Reframe fear as feedback.**

Instead of seeing fear as a stop sign, treat it as information. Ask, *"What is this fear trying to teach me about what I value?"* Often, fear shows up where your purpose is waiting to grow.

2. **Choose movement over paralysis.**

Don't wait for the perfect conditions to act—take one small step forward. Even the smallest motion creates momentum. Courage grows through motion, not meditation.

3. **Practice calm, not control.**

You can't control every outcome, but you can control your response. When chaos hits, take a breath before reacting. Center yourself. Calm is not weakness; it's quiet strength.

4. **Focus on what remains.**

When everything feels like it's falling apart, take stock of what's still standing—your values, resilience, and faith. That's your foundation. Build from there.

REAL COURAGE IS QUIET

Real courage rarely looks glamorous.

It's not always public or praised. It's often the unspoken victories, like forgiving when you'd rather fight, or believing again when your heart is still bruised. Courage is the mother who gets up after loss. It's the father who keeps providing, even when he's weary. It's the dreamer who tries one more time after every door has closed. I had to push through each time I was knocked down, each time a family member of mine passed away, each time I had to start over from a new job. Courage doesn't always roar. Sometimes, it's the sound of your feet hitting the floor in the morning, whispering, *"I'm still here."*

REFLECTION QUESTIONS

Where in your life is chaos testing your courage right now?

_____
_____
_____
_____
_____

What fear have you been waiting to overcome before you move forward? What if you moved *with* it instead?

_____
_____
_____
_____
_____

What does letting go look like for you, and what peace might be waiting on the other side?

_____
_____
_____
_____
_____
_____
_____

CLOSING THOUGHT

Courage in chaos is not about being unshaken, it's about refusing to stay broken. It's the decision to show up for your life, even when it hurts, even when it's unclear, even when you don't feel strong enough. The truth is, chaos doesn't define you; your choices in the middle of it do. Every time you choose courage over comfort, you become the proof that strength doesn't come from avoiding the storm, but from learning how to stand in the rain.

Pillar 3

Wisdom Through Waiting – Learning to Trust Divine Timing

Waiting is one of life's most difficult teachers. It tests our patience, challenges our faith, and confronts our desire for control. We live in a world that praises speed—fast results, instant success, overnight change—but real growth doesn't happen on demand. It unfolds in seasons. Wisdom through waiting means learning to trust that delay is not denial. It's realizing that the quiet seasons, the slow seasons, and even the painful pauses all serve a greater purpose—one that may not make sense until later.

THE SILENT CLASSROOM OF WAITING

Waiting is not wasted time; it's preparation time. It's in the silence between what you prayed for and what you see that your character is shaped. I can still remember the seasons in my life when I wanted answers right away, when I begged for doors to open, for people to change, for opportunities to appear. It felt like everyone else was moving forward while I was stuck at a red light that wouldn't turn green.

I learned that waiting doesn't mean nothing is happening. Sometimes, it's the space where everything is *becoming*. Like a seed buried in the soil, unseen but growing, your dreams are taking root in the dark. You can't always see the progress, but that doesn't mean growth isn't taking place. The seed doesn't rush, it simply trusts the process.

That's the kind of patience wisdom calls for.

THE PURPOSE OF THE PAUSE

When life slows down or feels like it's standing still, it's easy to panic. You start questioning yourself: *Did I take the wrong path? Did I miss my chance? Has God forgotten me?*

But often, the pause isn't punishment—it's protection. Sometimes, you're being held back from what's not ready for you yet, or what *you're* not yet ready for. Think about it this way: if you give a child the keys to a car before they've learned to drive, that gift becomes dangerous. Timing matters as much as the blessing itself. So maybe that job, opportunity, relationship, or breakthrough hasn't come yet, not because you're being overlooked, but because you're being *prepared*. The wait is not about making you weaker; it's about making you wiser. It teaches patience, discernment, and strength that instant gratification can never build.

LEARNING TO LIVE IN THE IN-BETWEEN

The in-between season—where one chapter is closing but the next hasn't opened—is often where people lose heart. It's where discouragement grows and comparison creeps in.

You start seeing others getting what you've been praying for, and suddenly your journey feels smaller. But wisdom through waiting reminds you that every person has their own timeline. Your pace has purpose. The sun and the moon don't compete; they shine when it's their time.

While you're waiting, life is still happening. Don't waste the waiting season wishing it away. Use it to develop yourself. Read. Learn. Heal. Grow. Strengthen what you'll need for where you're going. Waiting isn't about being idle; it's about being intentional.

PATIENCE AS A SUPERPOWER

We tend to think of patience as weakness, as if it means we're being passive or stuck. But patience is one of the strongest forces you can develop. It's controlled strength. It's the ability to stay grounded when everything in you wants to run ahead.

Patience says, *"I trust that what's mine will find me and I don't have to chase it to prove it."* When you cultivate that kind of patience, you stop making desperate decisions. You stop accepting less just because you're tired of waiting for more. You stop rushing into relationships, jobs, or environments that look good but aren't aligned with your growth.

Wisdom is knowing that not everything that comes quickly lasts, but what's built with patience endures.

HOW TO GAIN WISDOM THROUGH WAITING

Here are a few principles to help you navigate the waiting season with grace and strength:

1. Reframe the delay.

Instead of saying, *"Nothing is happening,"* ask, *"What is this season trying to teach me?"* Every delay carries a lesson, if you're willing to listen.

2. Focus on who you're becoming.

Waiting shifts your focus from what you want to *who you're becoming.* Character development is invisible at first, but it's the foundation for lasting success.

3. Replace anxiety with alignment.

Use waiting as a time to align your thoughts, goals, and spirit. Instead of forcing things to happen, align with the person you need to be for the next level.

4. Journal your journey.

Write about what you're learning, feeling, and observing. You'll be amazed at how much transformation happens in the stillness once you look back.

5. Celebrate small growth.

Even when you're not "there" yet, you're still moving. Every small step, every lesson learned, every day you didn't give up, that's progress worth celebrating.

WHAT WAITING REVEALS

Waiting reveals what we truly believe. It exposes whether we trust the process or just the results. It reveals if we're anchored in faith or driven by fear. When you're waiting and nothing seems to change, your emotions may whisper, *"It's not working."* But wisdom says, *"It's working in ways you can't yet see."* Think about a tree during winter. To the naked eye, it looks lifeless, but beneath the frozen ground, roots are deepening so when spring arrives, it can bloom stronger than before. That's what waiting does for your soul. It deepens your roots. It prepares you to sustain the growth that's coming.

REFLECTION QUESTIONS

What season of waiting are you currently in, and what might it be teaching you?

_____
_____
_____
_____

How do you usually respond to delays? With frustration or with faith?

_____
_____
_____
_____

What could you focus on developing in yourself while you wait?

_____
_____
_____
_____
_____
_____

CLOSING THOUGHT

Wisdom through waiting isn't about sitting still and doing nothing, it's about learning, listening, and preparing while you wait. Life's most meaningful moments often come after long seasons of uncertainty. Waiting is where endurance meets enlightenment and where patience gives birth to purpose. So, if you're in a season where nothing seems to be moving, take heart; maybe *you're* the one being moved. Growth doesn't always look like progress. Sometimes, it looks like peace in the middle of a pause. When you learn to wait well, you realize the wait was never a delay—it was divine direction.

Pillar 4

Grace for Growth – Becoming Better, Not Bitter

Growth is never gentle. It stretches, shakes, and sometimes shatters the old version of you so a wiser, stronger, freer version can emerge. But too often, instead of growing, we grieve the changes. We hold on to old identities, old hurts, and old expectations, and in doing so, we stop ourselves from becoming. Grace for growth means giving yourself permission to evolve. It's the ability to look at your past—every mistake, every heartbreak, every disappointment—and say, *"Even that served me."* Growth without grace turns into guilt, and guilt will keep you stuck in the very chapter you were meant to rise from.

THE BREAKING THAT BUILDS YOU

No one tells you how much growth hurts. They speak of transformation as if it's a pretty process, but real growth is gritty. It's the nights you cry quietly so no one sees your pain. It's the moments you question if you're doing enough, being enough, or healing fast enough.

Growth feels like loss because, in many ways, it is. You lose the comfort of who you were. You lose the need to please everyone. You lose the illusion of control. Yet, what you gain in return—peace, clarity, and self-respect—is worth every tear you shed.

Grace is what helps you survive that breaking. It's the gentle reminder that you're not behind; you're just becoming. It's the voice that says, *"You don't need to have it all figured out right now. You just need to keep showing up."*

The truth is, growth doesn't happen in one big moment—it happens in small, quiet decisions.

The decision:

- to forgive instead of fight.
- to rest instead of quit.
- to let go instead of cling.
- to move forward instead of replaying the pain.

Every time you choose growth over bitterness, you're rewriting your story.

THE GIFT OF SELF-COMPASSION

One of the greatest lessons in grace is learning to be kind to yourself while you're becoming.

Many people can extend compassion to others but struggle to give it to themselves. They hold onto guilt for years, replaying what they *"should have done differently,"* not realizing that they're punishing a version of themselves that didn't know what they know now. But you can't heal by hating yourself. You can't grow by shaming your past.

Grace invites you to forgive yourself, not to excuse what happened, but to free yourself from being defined by it.

When you give yourself grace, you start to see failure differently. You realize that falling short doesn't mean you're not capable; it means you're still human. Grace transforms "I failed" into "I learned." The moment you start showing yourself the same patience you give to others, you'll notice something powerful: healing starts to feel lighter. Growth starts to feel possible because you can't truly move forward while carrying the weight of unforgiveness, especially when that unforgiveness is toward yourself.

THE POWER OF PERSPECTIVE

Grace also changes how you view your journey. Instead of resenting the pain, you begin to see its purpose. You stop asking, *"Why did this happen to me?"* and start asking, *"What did this teach me?"* You begin to understand that every difficult experience was a teacher disguised as a trial.

The betrayal taught you boundaries.

The loss taught you gratitude.

The rejection taught you redirection.

The struggle taught you strength.

Grace shifts your perspective from victimhood to victory. It reminds you that everything that happened didn't happen *to* you, it happened *for* you. It's easy to let bitterness take root when life feels unfair. Bitterness says, *"They got away with it."* Grace says, *"I got away from it, and I'm still growing."* When you start to view your life through the lens of grace, you realize you haven't lost as much as you think. You've been refined, not ruined.

HOW TO GROW WITH GRACE

Growth with grace isn't just about enduring change, it's about embracing it with intention and self-awareness. Here are some ways to practice grace as you grow:

1. Release perfection.

You don't have to have every detail of your life perfectly together. Growth is messy. Mistakes are part of mastery. Give yourself space to be human.

2. Reflect before you react.

Grace pauses. Before snapping in anger or drowning in regret, stop and ask: *"What's this really teaching me?"* The pause itself is growth.

3. **Practice gratitude.**

Even in painful seasons, look for what's still good. Gratitude transforms frustration into fuel and bitterness into blessing.

4. **Speak gently to yourself.**

Your self-talk shapes your growth. When you fall short, don't say, *"I'm a failure."* Say, *"I'm still learning."* What you repeat, you believe, so let your words build, not break.

5. **Surround yourself with grace-givers.**

Growth thrives in environments where grace is modeled. Spend time with people who challenge you, but also nurture you; those who see your progress, not just your past.

WHEN GROWTH GETS LONELY

One of the hardest parts about growth is that not everyone will understand it. Some people preferred the version of you that tolerated nonsense, stayed small, or settled for less. When you start changing, they'll say you've changed, as if that's a bad thing. But it's not. It's necessary. You will outgrow environments that no longer match your mindset. You will lose connections that cannot handle your new boundaries. You will walk away from situations that once defined you. That's what evolution looks like, and grace helps you do it without resentment. It teaches you to bless what you leave behind, not because it didn't hurt, but because it helped you grow. Every closed door, every goodbye, every loss shaped the person you're becoming. Grace gives you the courage to say, *"Thank you for the lesson. I'm ready for what's next."*

REFLECTION QUESTIONS

What situations in your life are currently stretching you to grow?

_____
_____
_____
_____
_____
_____
_____

Are you being kind to yourself in this process, or are you being your own critic?

_____
_____
_____
_____
_____
_____
_____

Who or what do you need to forgive to move forward freely?

_____
_____
_____
_____

Write down three things you've learned from your hardest seasons. Then, beside each one, write how it made you better. You'll begin to see how grace has been guiding you all along.

CLOSING THOUGHT

Grace for growth is what allows you to heal without hate, to evolve without ego, and to rise without resentment. It's what turns pain into power and transition into transformation.

When you give yourself permission to grow with grace, you stop measuring your progress by perfection and start measuring it by peace. You begin to trust that every uncomfortable season is carving out a stronger, wiser, more resilient version of you. You are not who you were, and that's something to celebrate. Growth doesn't mean you've changed too much; it means you've finally started to become who you were always meant to be.

Pillar 5

Purpose Through Pain – Turning Wounds into Wisdom

Pain has a way of making us question everything—our strength, worth, future, and even our faith in ourselves. Yet, if you trace the path of your greatest growth, you'll notice something powerful: the lessons that shaped you most came wrapped in discomfort.

Pain, though unwanted, is often life's greatest teacher. It demands your attention. It interrupts your comfort. It exposes what needs healing, and it invites you to rise above what tried to break you. But purpose through pain isn't about glorifying the struggle, it's about *extracting meaning from it*. It's about taking the parts of your story that once made you feel ashamed or defeated, and allowing them to become your source of strength and service to others. You've endured things that would have crushed a weaker spirit, but you're still standing. That means your pain wasn't sent to destroy you; it was sent to develop you.

THE REFINING POWER OF PAIN

When life hurts, our first instinct is to escape it. We run from pain because it's uncomfortable, raw, and unpredictable. But in running, we miss what pain is trying to reveal.

Pain refines you the way fire refines gold, not to punish you but to remove what no longer belongs. Every time you walk through hardship, something within you is being purified: your motives, priorities, and perception.

Think about it: the person you were before the heartbreak, the disappointment, or the setback, is not the same person reading these words now. The pain stripped away the illusions. It revealed your strength. It sharpened your discernment. It taught you boundaries, balance, and bravery. Sometimes pain shows you what you didn't know you could survive. It gives you evidence of your resilience. It forces you to dig deep and discover that you have more power within you than you ever imagined. Pain is a refiner, not a reminder of your weakness, but a revelation of your strength.

FINDING PURPOSE IN WHAT TRIED TO BREAK YOU

Every wound has a story, and within every story lies a lesson that someone else needs. When you begin to view your pain as a platform, not a prison, everything shifts. Your story—the one you've been trying to hide or rewrite—might be the very thing someone else needs to see the light at the end of their tunnel. The purpose of pain isn't just survival; it's transformation. It's learning to take what hurt you and use it to heal others. It's learning that nothing you went through was wasted. You might not see it yet, but there is divine strategy hidden in every scar.

That heartbreak taught you self-worth.

That loss taught you gratitude.

That betrayal taught you discernment.

That disappointment taught you faith.

You may not have chosen the pain, but you can choose what to do with it now. You can either let it harden you, or you can let it heighten you.

When you start turning your wounds into wisdom, you begin to walk differently. You stop needing validation and start carrying revelation. You realize that every painful chapter was a setup for the purpose you're now stepping into.

FROM PAIN TO POWER: HOW TO TRANSFORM YOUR STORY

Transforming pain into purpose doesn't happen overnight. It's a process of reflection, acceptance, and redirection. It's both emotional and intentional. Here's how to begin that transformation:

1. Feel it fully.

Don't rush your healing. Too many people try to skip the grieving process, thinking strength means silence. But real strength is allowing yourself to feel without losing hope.

2. Learn from it.

Ask yourself: *"What did this pain teach me?"* Every experience, no matter how painful, has a lesson. Sometimes it's about people, sometimes it's about you.

3. Reframe it.

Instead of saying, *"This broke me,"* say, *"This built me."* The language you use about your pain determines how it lives within you.

4. Share it.

There's healing in storytelling. Whether through writing, speaking, or simple conversations, sharing your journey helps you release the weight of it and empowers others to heal too.

5. Serve through it.

Your purpose often hides behind your pain. The same comfort you once needed becomes the comfort you now give; helping others transforms suffering into significance.

LESSONS FROM THE JOURNEY

When you start to see your pain through the lens of purpose, life begins to make more sense. You stop asking, *"Why me?"* and start declaring, *"Why not me?"* Because only someone who has walked through the fire can help others find their way out. The truth is, the greatest leaders, healers, and innovators often come from the deepest wounds. They don't speak from theory, they speak from experience. That's what gives their words power.

So if you've been wondering why you had to endure so much, remember this: pain prepared you for the platform. You had to be crushed in order to carry compassion. You had to be broken to understand how to build others. Your suffering gave birth to your strength.

REFLECTION QUESTIONS

Write down one painful experience that changed you.

_____
_____
_____
_____
_____
_____
_____

List three lessons that came out of that season.

_____
_____
_____
_____
_____
_____

Ask yourself: *"How can I use what I've learned to help someone else?"*

_____
_____
_____
_____
_____
_____

These questions aren't just reflective, they're transformative. They help you move from victim to vessel, from wounded to wise. The most powerful stories are not the ones that hide the pain, but the ones that transform it.

CLOSING THOUGHT

Pain is inevitable, but purpose is a choice. You don't get to control every storm, but you do get to choose what you build from its aftermath. Your scars are not signs of shame, they are symbols of survival. They tell the world, *"I've been through the fire, but I came out refined."* When you find purpose in pain, you stop living as a product of what happened and start living as proof that healing is possible. So, as you turn the page from this chapter to the next, remember: your wounds were never meant to define you; they were meant to *design* you. Your story now has the power to lead others out of their own darkness into light.

You are not what hurt you.

You are what healed through you.

And that is your purpose.

Final Reflection

Life doesn't hand us a manual on how to survive the storms; it gives us storms that teach us how to survive. Every tear, every test, and every turning point have been part of shaping who you've become today. You are not the same person who began this book. You have faced your reflection, embraced your truth, and discovered that even in your weakest moments, there was strength waiting to emerge.

The journey through pain, faith, and growth is not a straight path; it twists, it bends, it breaks you open, and then rebuilds you stronger. That's what resilience truly is: the sacred ability to bend without breaking, to fall and still find the courage to rise.

Through these pages, you've walked the framework: the Five Pillars of Fierce Resilience. Each one is more than a concept; it's a way of life. They are not steps you climb once and leave behind; they are truths you return to over and over again. Together, they form the foundation for unshakeable strength and unstoppable growth.

Here is a summary of each pillar that you can read daily!

THE FIVE PILLARS OF RESILIENCE SUMMARIZED FOR DAILY READING

FAITH BEYOND FEELINGS

Faith was never about knowing every answer; it was about trusting through uncertainty. You've learned that emotions fluctuate, but faith anchors. When life feels unstable, your belief keeps you grounded. You now understand that faith is not just spiritual; it's practical power. It's the calm voice in chaos that whispers, *"Keep moving, this won't break you."*

When your feelings deceive you, let your faith remind you: the same God who carried you through the past will carry you through what's ahead.

COURAGE IN CHAOS

Courage isn't loud; sometimes it's silent endurance. It's showing up, even when no one claps. It's facing what frightens you and saying, *"I'm still here."* You've learned that courage is built in the moments that test your will.

Even in chaos, you have the power to choose peace. You've realized that bravery doesn't mean you aren't afraid; it means you move forward anyway. And now, every obstacle before you is no longer a stop sign, but a signal that you're stepping into your next level.

WISDOM THROUGH WAITING

Waiting taught you what rushing never could. It shaped your patience, deepened your trust, and stretched your vision. You discovered that delays are not denials; they are divine redirections. In the stillness, you found strength. In the waiting, you learned wisdom. Life's pauses were never empty; they were sacred. They were molding you for moments that required a steadier heart and clearer focus. You can now say, *"I may not be where I want to be, but I'm exactly where I'm meant to be right now."*

GRACE FOR GROWTH

Growth is never graceful, but you've learned to give yourself grace through the process. You've learned that healing takes time, that transformation takes patience, and that you don't have to be perfect to be progressing. Grace reminded you that mistakes are not final; they're formative. Every misstep was an invitation to start again with wisdom. You have learned to release the weight of shame and walk lighter, freer, and more aligned with who you are becoming. You no longer apologize for growing. You celebrate it because growth is proof that you are evolving into the best version of yourself.

PURPOSE THROUGH PAIN

Pain no longer defines you; it refines you. What once wounded you now empowers you. You've learned to transform your pain into purpose, your struggle into strength, and your scars into stories that heal others.

You are now living proof that brokenness can become brilliance. That what was meant to destroy you became the very thing that developed your destiny.

Your pain gave birth to your passion, and your purpose is no longer hidden; it's alive within you, burning brighter than the battles you've overcome.

Why I Wrote This Book

I am a grown woman who has walked through the darkest nights of her youth and lived to see the sunrise of strength. I chose to write this book to inspire others—especially women—to rise above pain and turn their trials into triumph.

Countless women in the world have suffered in silence—emotionally, physically, and even through sexual assault—at the hands of those who believed they could control them. To my sisters, mothers, and grandmothers, I say this: let us stand together in unity and sisterhood. Let us show the world the power we possess when we rise as one.

Many are afraid to tell their stories, but I challenge you to speak your truth. Do not be silent. You have a voice, and your story carries power. You have within you the strength to rebuild, to heal, and to inspire others to do the same.

The struggle is indeed real, but so is your strength.

You have survived things you never thought you could. You have endured storms that should have broken you. Yet, here you are, not just surviving, but transforming.

This book is not simply about hardship; it's about victory. It's a reminder that your story still has power, your purpose still matters, and your life still has meaning. So, hold your head high. Walk with courage. Lead with grace. And remember: you are the embodiment of fierce resilience. You are living proof that nothing real can be destroyed; not your faith, not your hope, not your fire.

Stop chasing what your mind desires and begin to pursue what your soul truly needs. Life is not about the pain you've endured, but about the strength you've discovered through it. So stand tall. Keep believing. Keep shining because your story—your journey—may be the very light that leads someone else out of the dark.

You have within you the ability to create, to overcome, and to transform.
You are capable of more than you know.
So write. Speak. Live. Inspire.

The world is waiting for your voice.

About the Author

Lavern Carr is a woman of remarkable resilience, faith, and purpose. Her life reflects a deep compassion and an unwavering belief in the power of perseverance. Through personal challenges, she has cultivated strength, integrity, and a spirit of growth that inspires those around her.

A devoted family person, Lavern embodies generosity, loyalty, and positivity, showing that faith and love can guide us through life's toughest trials. Her journey is a living testament to the truth that through faith and determination, all things are possible. With a heart anchored in resilience and a commitment to personal growth, Lavern inspires others to navigate life's challenges with courage, integrity, and compassion, turning obstacles into opportunities for transformation.

www.ingramcontent.com/pod-product-compliance
Lightning Source LLC
Chambersburg PA
CBHW071212160426
43196CB00011B/2265